WORDPRESS UNBOXED

THE SIMPLE, JARGON-FREE GUIDE TO SETTING UP YOUR FIRST WORDPRESS WEBSITE

P. Teague

Copyright © 2017 by Paul Teague (writing as P.Teague) & Clixeo Publishing

No part of this book may be reproduced, stored in retrieval systems, or transmitted by any means, electronic, mechanical, photocopying, recorded or otherwise without written permission from the author.

Disclaimer

Some of the services recommended in this book will earn me a small affiliate income if you click on certain links and go on to purchase. I only recommend products and services which I personally use. Please read my disclosure notice at http://www.clixeo.com/disclosure/ for full information.

All the information in this book was up to date at the time of publication. Due to the ever-changing nature of the web, some of the screen shots may differ slightly from what you see in your own account. ***Please note that this book is sold as-is, without the provision or expectation of support or technical assistance.***

Wordpress is a registered Trademark of The Wordpress Foundation, which does not endorse, support or sponsor the content of this book in any way. All opinions expressed are those of the author.

WORDPRESS UNBOXED VIDEO

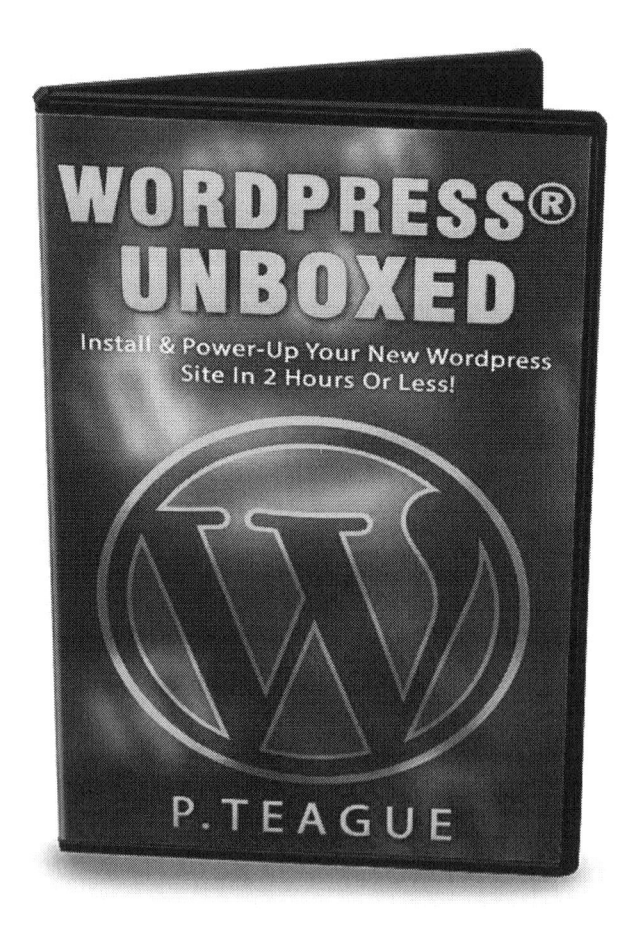

Grab your free 1-hour Wordpress video walk-through at

https://wp-unboxed.com/FREE

Why I Wrote This Book

I first used Wordpress in 2008, as a complete blogging novice.

Before that, I'd dabbled with Blogger.com which, in those days was not as well developed as it is now.

I'd never written a blog post before, I hadn't got a clue what I was going to write about and – if I'm totally honest – I was a little bit embarrassed about people reading my posts.

My first blog started out life as laptopmanpaul.co.uk (thewaybackmachine.com has it listed as August 2008) and over the years it has evolved, of course, becoming what it is now - PaulTeague.com, the main platform for my online work.

In fact, at the time of writing, that blog is about to undergo another metamorphosis as I begin to move more of my posts into the realms of writing and digital publishing.

Since 2008 I can confidently say that I have installed Wordpress well over 100 times (probably many more, but I don't want to exaggerate the numbers) and I have built a massive variety of sites, from complex membership sites to simple sales page sites, and, of course, my own blog.

I have taught Wordpress techniques to many business people and online entrepreneurs, face-to-face and via webinars, and I have managed Wordpress plugin software projects.

I use and love Wordpress. To me, there is no other choice or option when it comes to setting up your online platform.

I hope that by the time you have read this book, you will share that enthusiasm and want to dive straight in and get started.

Paul Teague

Brought to you by

clixeo

What This Book Will Help You Do

I have written this book with one intention in mind.

When you have read it, and done the things that I show you *exactly* how to do, you will have your own Wordpress blog and you will know how to use it.

But let me be specific about that.

This book will show you:

1: How to install Wordpress, on free hosting or on paid hosting. I will show you how you can do *everything* completely free of charge if you need to do it that way.

2: How to choose a free or paid theme for Wordpress. You'll have a great looking site in no time.

3: How to set up your new Wordpress site the right way.

4: How to create posts and pages, and the difference between the two.

5: How to use tags and categories, and the differences between the two.

6: How to find and install plugins.

7: A selection of the best Wordpress plugins to use.

8: How to set up the SEO basics on your new blog to make sure that you can be found in the search engines.

9: Essential tips to keep your Wordpress site safe from hackers.

10: How to add images and videos to your blog posts.

11: Which free plugins to use to get your Wordpress site firing on all cylinders.

12: Where to find some of the hidden features of Wordpress.

13: How to fine tune Wordpress to get it performing the way it should for blogging success.

14: How to use Wordpress widgets and menus on your new blog.

Contents

Chapter 1: Why Wordpress? - 5

Chapter 2: Installing Wordpress for Free - 9

Chapter 3: The Recommended Way to Install Wordpress - 18

Chapter 4: Getting to Know the Wordpress Dashboard - 36

Chapter 5: Wordpress Settings - 43

Chapter 6: Creating Posts and Pages - 60

Chapter 7: Using Media Files - 80

Chapter 8: Changing the Appearance of Your Blog - 104

Chapter 9: Wordpress Plugins - 116

Chapter 10: Essential Wordpress Plugins - 126

Chapter 11: Wordpress Miscellany - 140

Chapter 12: Other Useful Things To Do In Siteground - 154

What Next with Wordpress? - 162

About The Author - 164

Other Resources from Paul Teague - 165

Chapter 1: Why Wordpress?

So, why use Wordpress anyway? why not just go for the easy option and use Blogger?

I've answered this question many times, and the final decision lies with you of course, but the benefits of choosing Wordpress are very clear to me as an established user:

Reason 1: It's free! Need I say more?

Reason 2: Once you've got the basics, it's easy to use. Seriously. Can you create a listing in eBay? If the answer is 'yes,' then you can master Wordpress quickly.

Reason 3: It's easy to update at any time. Need a responsive theme so that your site displays properly on tablets and phones? It's sorted in a minute with Wordpress.

Reason 4: It's scalable. You can use it 100% free on day 1. As your business grows you can add new pages, get a proper web address for it, then move it to paid hosting. As your business explodes, you can move to virtual servers, have a blogging staff writing 20 posts a day and cope with millions of visitors. You can easily migrate it to a new web host too, so you're never trapped in a 'hostage' situation where you have to stay with a particular developer or web host because they control all of your web content.

Reason 5: You'll be in good company. Forbes, CNN, eBay, Sony, Techcrunch and Katy Perry all use Wordpress. Need some more big company names to convince you? Check out http://en.wordpress.com/notable-users/

Reason 6: Wordpress makes SEO (search engine optimization) a breeze. SEO is your website's ability to rank well in the search engines. These days, that usually means Google. Using Wordpress, you can get all the SEO basics right without having to spend all of your cash on expensive agencies. And yes, I will tell you how to set it all up in this book.

Reason 7: Wordpress is Open Source. What that means is that thousands of developers all over the world contribute to make it what it is. That ensures that you get the best minds, the best solutions and it's always bang up to date and cutting edge. Oh, and did I mention, you get all the benefits of that effort and expertise for free?

Reason 8: Wordpress is extremely well supported, which means that if you do ever run into a problem, the answer will be easy to find. Just do a search for 'Free Wordpress Tutorial' and take a look at the results that come in. Note too, the number of YouTube step-by-step videos that you can access. There is so much free help out there, it's very unlikely that you'll ever run into an issue that can't be solved.

Reason 9: Wordpress has lots of add-ons. In 'Wordpress-speak' these are called plugins. You'll learn to love plugins, I guarantee it. Want to add videos to your site?

Simple, there's a free plugin for that. Want to link up Wordpress with your newsletter service? No problem, there's a plugin for that. In fact, there are many, many plugins for that. Want to take payments via Paypal on your website and create a record of customers? Easy, there's a plugin for that. Whatever you want to do on Wordpress, there's usually a plugin for it. And if there isn't? What if you want something really obscure on your site? It's really easy to get one made because there are so many developers who provide that service.

Reason 10: Millions of people are using Wordpress already. Would they be using it if it was a pile of junk? Of course not! I said at the beginning of this book that there are many other alternatives to Wordpress. But why do you think that millions of people – including massive corporations – use it? Because it's brilliant, that's why. The statistics for Wordpress are changing all the time, so I'm not going to quote them here as they'll soon be out of date. Usually, because those numbers of users just keep increasing as more and more users flock to use this amazing software. If you want your eyes to pop out with some amazing Wordpress statistics, read the stats page on https://wordpress.com/activity/.

What's The Difference Between a Blog And A Website?

I get asked this question a lot, so it's worth addressing it here I think.

A traditional website is static, in that you set it up once and you won't see a lot of changes after that.

A static website usually has a welcome page accompanied by 'Contact Us,' 'About Us,' 'Where We're Located' and maybe a few other basics.

However, once all that is in place, not much changes on the site.

This is the 'old-fashioned' way of doing things on the web.

A blog, however, is a living, breathing, organic website.

It will have all those basics, of course, things like 'Contact Us' and 'About Us', but the big difference is that it is regularly updated with new, exciting and relevant content.

This content is made in the form of 'posts' or updates.

There is something very special about blogs though that supercharges these posts.

Blogs use something called RSS (Really Simple Syndication) which allows interested readers to subscribe to your web content and get it delivered directly to them via email, software services or feeds.

This is a great description of RSS:

It is a way to easily distribute a list of headlines, update notices, and sometimes content to a wide number of people. It is used by computer programs that organize those headlines and notices for easy reading.

Source: http://rss.softwaregarden.com/aboutrss.html

So, in very simple terms, if you want to create regular content and stand the very best chance of getting it read and 'out there,' you need to use a blog.

And if you're going to use a blog, you need to use Wordpress, because this amazing software will make the process of creating and sharing fabulous content a thing of wonderful simplicity.

Why Not Blogger?

I want to be very clear that in spite of my complete commitment and enthusiasm for Wordpress, I am not for one minute putting down any of the competitors.

I used Blogger before I used Wordpress, it must have been way back in 2008.

But I very quickly ran into limitations on Blogger, which made me explore further.

I have experimented in the past with Drupal, Mambo, Joomla, and Moodle, as well as some others which I have long since forgotten, but I kept coming back to Wordpress.

I recently did some guest blogging on a Blogger site and was interested to see how much it has changed since I last used it.

It was great; it's come a long way.

But you know what? I was going to share a link to those posts to show you what I'd done on Blogger.

But the owners of that site have converted it to Wordpress since I wrote those posts!

Why? Because all great bloggers know that you have to be using Wordpress if you're a serious player.

So save yourself the pain of the inevitable learning process if you choose any of the alternatives, opt for Wordpress from Day One, and there will be no looking back.

Wordpress.org or Wordpress.com?

This is the second most common question that I am asked, and again, we need to deal with it from the outset.

All Wordpress sites are not created equal.

Wordpress has its own Blogger 'lookalike,' and it can be found at https://wordpress.com/

It's really important that you understand the difference between these two Wordpress options and that you use the right one.

The Wordpress service that you need to use is https://wordpress.org/.

Now, Wordpress.org *is* the more complicated of the options, but please believe me when I advise you not to take the simplest route with Wordpress.com.

Wordpress.com is just like Blogger, Wordpress does all the hard work for you, with the hosting and URL, and you just do the creative stuff, like creating content.

There's a very big 'but' here, though.

The BIG problem with Blogger, Wordpress.com and other similar 'ready-made' options is that you don't control the content.

It sits on the Wordpress (or Blogger) servers, and you're stuck there, restricted by their site terms and conditions and also by the limitations of the service itself.

You get a very restricted choice of plugins and themes; you can't do all of the cool and amazing things that you can do in Wordpress.org.

Please trust me when I tell you that, even if you opt for Wordpress.com, you'll regret it in future when your blog takes off, and you'll wish that you just put it in Wordpress.org in the first place.

I did exactly that.

It's too long ago for me to recall the specific order in which I did it all now, but I moved from Blogger.com to Wordpress.com – via Drupal, Mambo, Joomla and the rest – and ended up at Wordpress.org.

Virtually all serious – and amateur – bloggers do.

So save yourself the trouble and inconvenience of making changes down the line, and get it right from the get-go by using Wordpress.org.

By the way, if you're using Blogger or Wordpress.com already, don't worry. All is not lost.

Wordpress is excellent; it allows you to import your blogging content from 3rd parties, simply and speedily.

That also applies to the reverse, in the very unlikely scenario that you can't stand Wordpress, you can easily switch to another service if you want to.

(There goes a flying pig, by the way, I always see one whenever I mention the possibility of hating Wordpress.)

Import options include Blogger, Tumblr, Joomla, Movable Type and Drupal to name just a few.

You'll find the full list at http://codex.wordpress.org/Importing_Content.

If you've just taken a look at https://wordpress.org/ and seen the words 'download' and 'install,' and you're about to run a mile, don't worry!

We don't have to do anything technical here.

Sure, you can install Wordpress the hard way if you really want to.

But I won't be showing you how to do that, even though I've done it many times because I want you to see how easy this is.

I do not want you bamboozled with tech talk and geek overload; I want you up-and-running on Wordpress as soon as possible, and with the least possible damage to your bank balance.

So let's get on with that straight away.

Chapter 2: Installing Wordpress for Free

Now we get to the good bit!

I love this part when I'm teaching people who are new to Wordpress because they just can't believe how fast this really is.

We do need to look at a few things first though, because you have to make a decision at this stage.

You can use Wordpress completely free of charge if you want to.

You don't even have to enter your credit card details to get started.

Is that the way I'd recommend it's done?

The answer is 'no,' I definitely *would not* recommend that you do this completely free.

However, whether you have zero budget or a small budget, one thing I can guarantee you is that you definitely *will not* need a large budget to use Wordpress.

You won't even need a medium budget.

My **recommended** way to use Wordpress is to:

- Use paid-for web hosting (but it's *very* inexpensive)

- Pay for your own domain name, i.e., http://mybusiness.com

I'll mention where you can access free Wordpress hosting for free, just in case it's handy.

Free Wordpress: My Preferred Free Option
This option involves the following:

- No bespoke URL or web link

- Ad-free and cost-free hosting

The service that I'm going to recommend for this is https://www.000webhost.com/

OooWebhost.com is genuinely free (they will encourage you to go for their paid for service, of course, they have to make a living!), there are no banner adverts and it does everything that you need it to do.

In particular, it will auto install Wordpress for you.

No software to download, no databases to create, it's just one click, and you're away!

A Quick Word About Domain Names

What most people want when they go online is a nice domain name or URL such as http://myname.com or http://mybusiness.com.

When you go 100% free, you're not going to get this.

It's one of the disadvantages of using services like Blogger or Wordpress.com too.

You get saddled with a web address that looks like this:

- http://paulteague-uk.blogspot.co.uk/

- http://pault23.wordpress.com/

(Yes, those are two of my very old and unloved accounts - proof of my activity on both Blogger and Wordpress.com.)

Those web addresses are what are known as subdomains.

The main domains are blogspot.co.uk and wordpress.com.

You get to create what's called a subdomain, effectively piggy-backing off somebody else's domain name.

As you can see, they're not very nice web links.

That's why I'd always recommend that you do the job properly and buy a great domain name.

So, in the case of 000webhost.com, we're also going to get saddled with a rather ugly subdomain when we take the 100% free option.

Registering Your Free 000webhost Account

Step 1: Go to https://www.000webhost.com/ and click on the Free Sign-Up button.

Step 2: Complete the simple registration form:

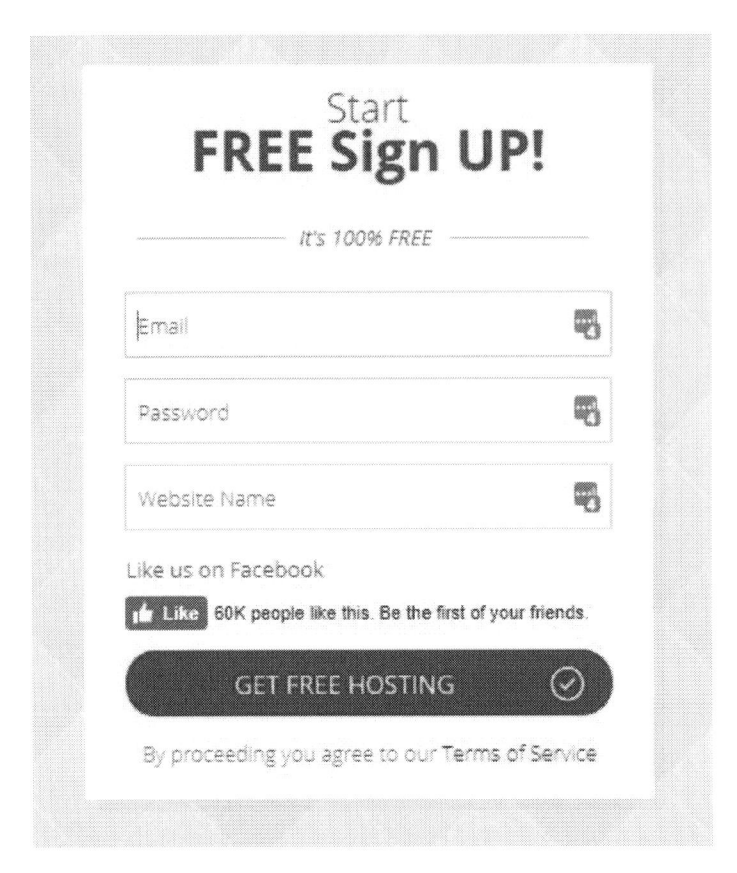

Come up with a decent website name ... your URL will be in the format https://**WEBSITENAME**.ooowebhostapp.com/

Step 3: You'll be asked to verify your email address – you'll have to do that before you can use the site.

It might take a little while to arrive, so please be patient!

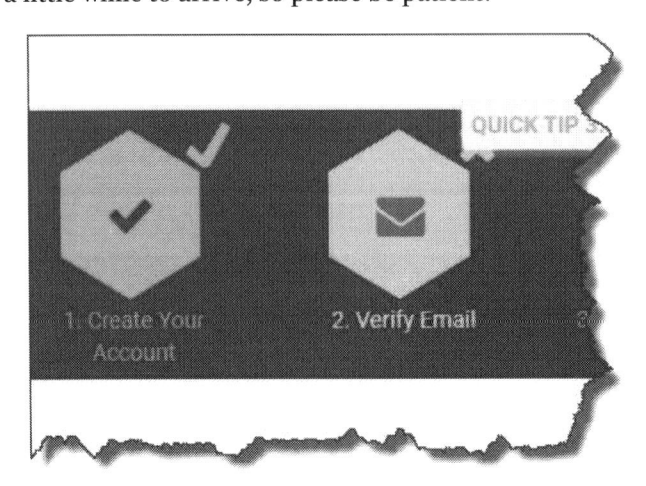

This is what the verification email will look like when it arrives – just click the **Verify email** button:

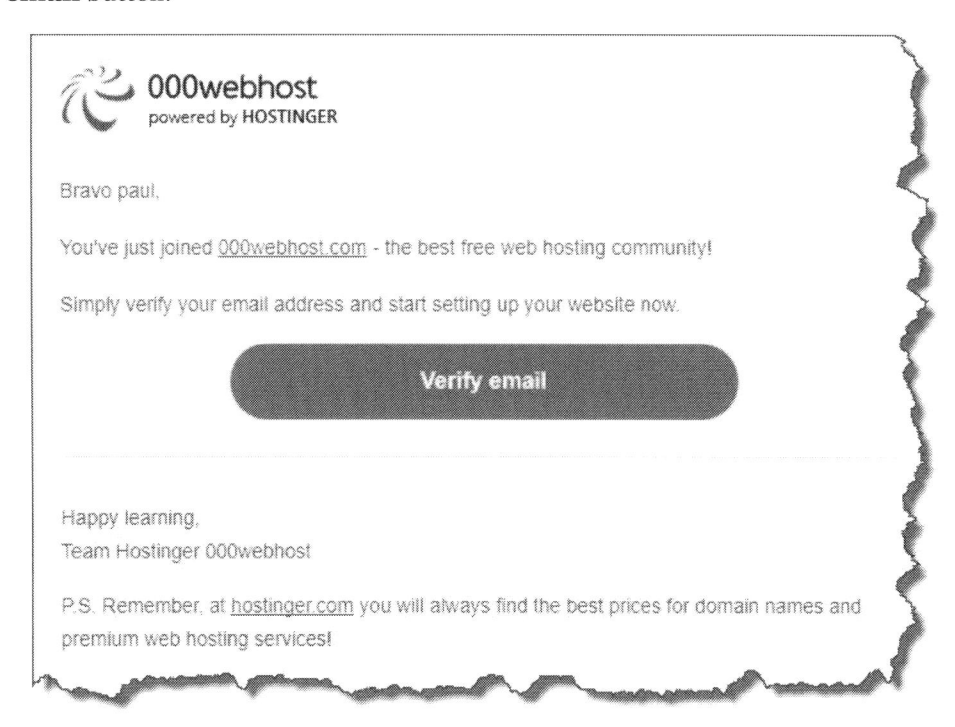

Step 4: Once you've completed the process successfully, you'll see this confirmation message.

Click on that red **Manage website** button to continue:

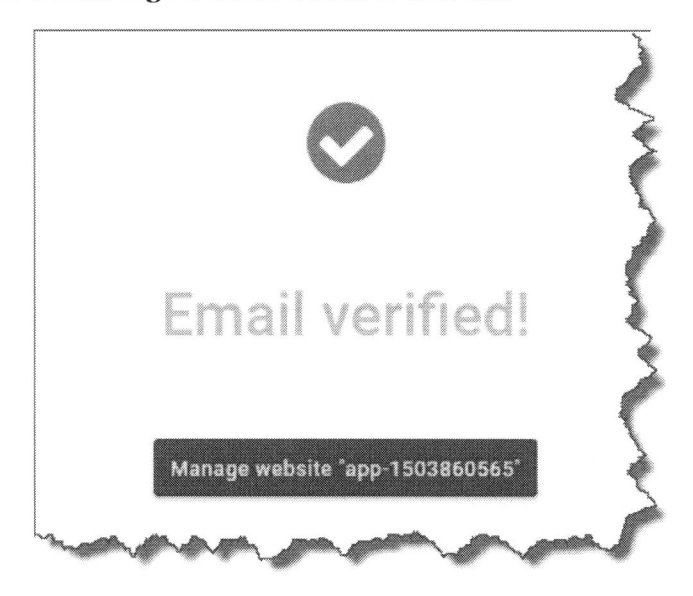

Until you complete the email confirmation process, you will not be able to continue creating your Wordpress site:

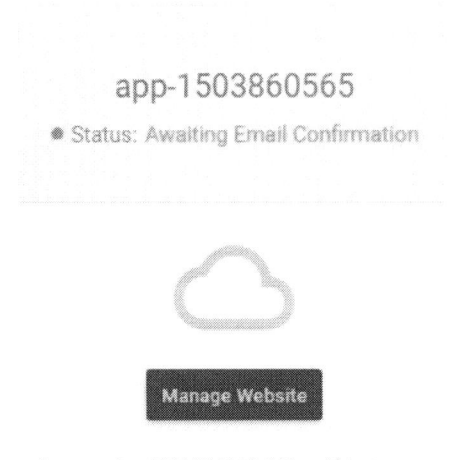

Step 5: Once everything is good to go, either of those **Manage website** buttons will take you to the screen below:

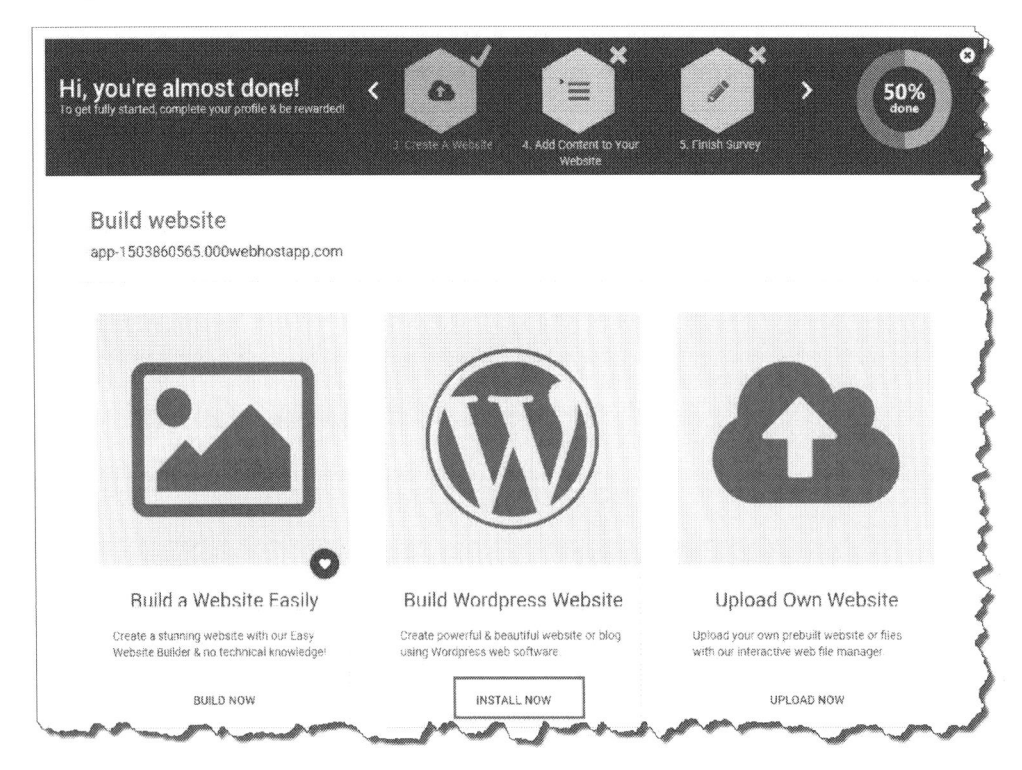

Head for the **Build Wordpress Website** area and click on that **Install Now** button.

Step 6: You now have to create a username and a password for your Wordpress site.

Important note! Do not use admin as your username.

Evil hacker types know that you're likely to do this and they're ready for you.

Instead, use something that isn't obvious:

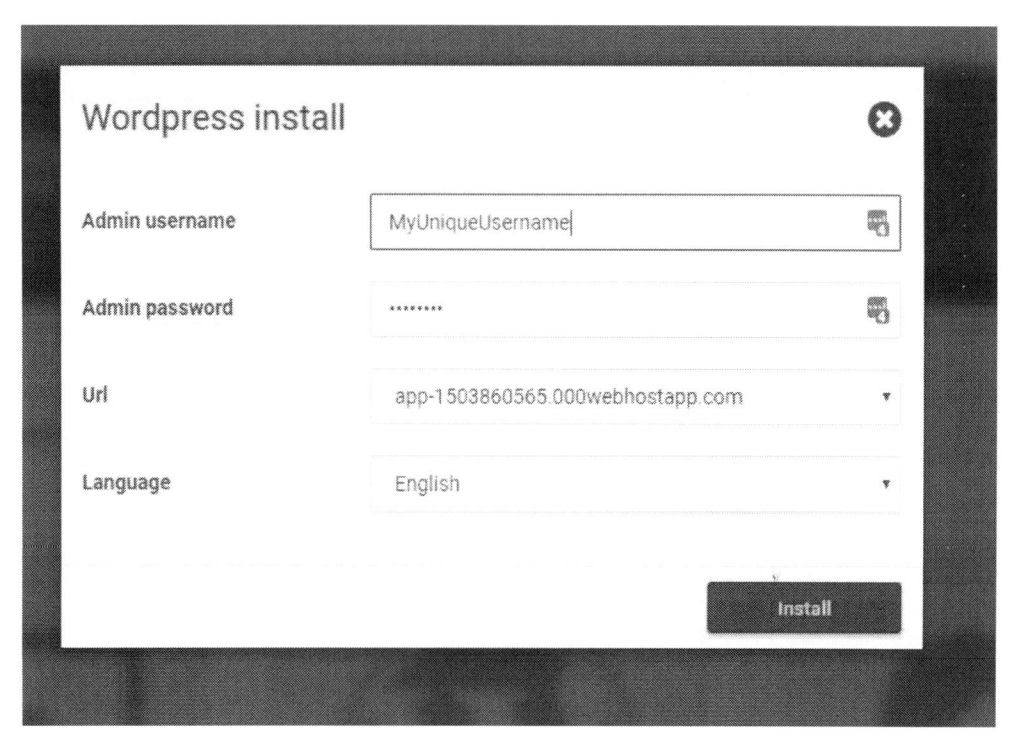

Make a note of your username and password, then click the red **Install** button.

Step 7: Do not interrupt the next process – your Wordpress site is being installed:

Step 8: Be patient with the installation process, you'll get a confirmation like the one below once it's completed:

Congratulations, it's ready!

Your Wordpress is now ready for configuration.

Go to configuration page

Step 9: Now we need to login to our brand new blog.

You'll see the Wordpress login form now:

Username or Email Address

MyUniqueUsername

Password

••••••••

Remember Me   Log In

Lost your password?

← Back to app-1503860565

Use the username and password that you (hopefully) jotted down a few moments ago.

Then click the **Login** button.

If you forget your password, just click on **Lost your password?** and reset it.

Step 10: You will now be taken to the Wordpress admin interface.

It will be cluttered up at first with this big promo for Hostinger.

Just click the small x as shown below and it will disappear:

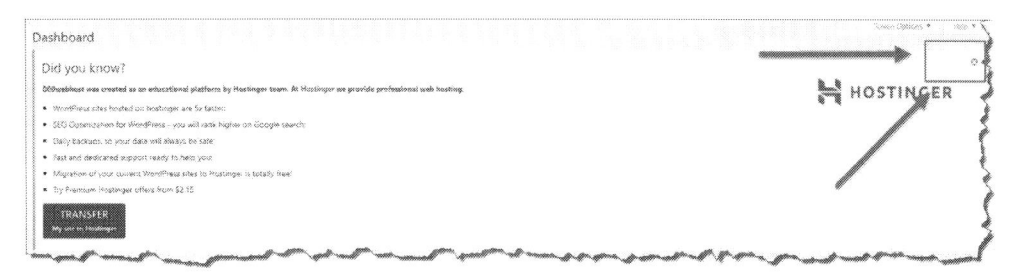

Step 11: This is what your Wordpress Admin area looks like now:

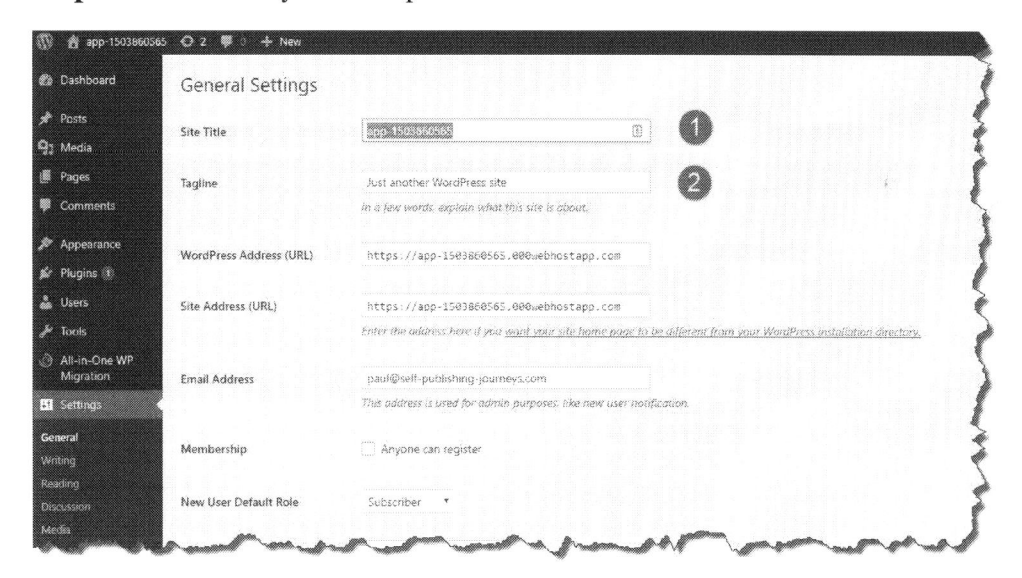

You need to add something meaningful in the Site Title [1] and Tagline [2] areas.

Site Title is exactly that, tagline should be a catchy sentence explaining what your site is about.

Step 12: This is what your blog looks like to the public (this may vary in appearance to the one on the next page if 000webhost alters its default theme):

There's nothing there at the moment because we haven't created any content yet, but everything that you need to create an amazing Wordpress blog has been done already.

That's as hard as it gets, everything else is simple by comparison.

If you ever want to reset or delete that Wordpress blog, head for the ooowebhost settings:

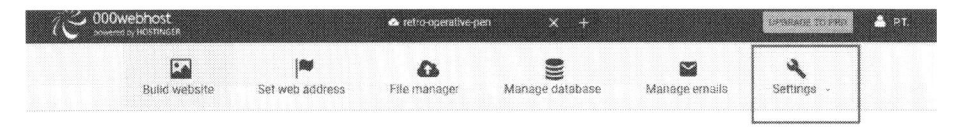

Select **General** in that setting menu, and click [1] to reset and [2] to delete:

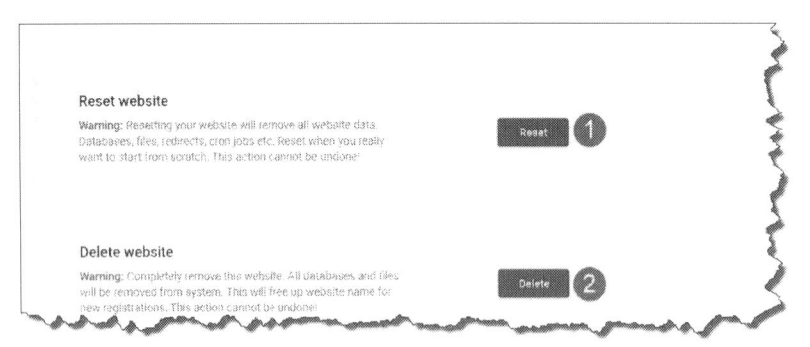

What Now?

Congratulations, you now have a 100% free of charge Wordpress blog.

Easy when you know how, isn't it?

You need to read the next section to see the *best* way to set up paid for Wordpress blog or, if you're staying with the free option, skip ahead to Chapter 4 to get your full introduction to the Wordpress Dashboard.

Chapter 3: The Recommended Way to Install Wordpress

I won't beat around the bush on this topic; there is no doubt in my mind that creating a completely free Wordpress account is <u>not</u> the best way to do things.

I don't like using horrible domain names, I don't like using subdomains (unless they're mine) and I think it gives a poor image of your business.

This is 'tough love' from me. You *can* do things for free, but when you run a business, sometimes you have to cough up a small amount of cash.

Compare the $50 or so that we're about to spend on basic web hosting with the expense of setting up a bricks and mortar shop.

There's rent, business rates, electricity, gas, fixtures and fittings, stock and staff before we even open the doors.

There is nothing as cost effective as an online business, and I really do recommend that you do spend a small amount of money to do things correctly.

There are very few barriers to entry with an online business, so if you really do have a zero budget, use the free option, if that's not the case, please do it this way.

Choosing a Web Host

There are many web hosting services available.

I'm going to recommend the one that I use myself because:

1 – I've used it happily for several years now

2 – I use it on more than 15 Wordpress sites and find it simple and reliable

3 – I use it for teaching because it's cheap, straightforward and the support is good

4 – It is used very widely in the internet marketing industry

5 – As an existing user I can give you a discount to get you started

I use Siteground for my own web hosting, and that's what I'll be using in this step-by-step guide.

Whatever you decide to use, for the sake of simplicity, always make sure that it uses **cPanel with QuickInstall** or **Softaculous** as that simplified interface will make your online life so much easier.

If you're not sure, ask via the service's helpdesk before you buy.

This is the link that you need to take you to the registration page shown in the image below https://www.siteground.com/wordpress-hosting.htm or, if you're happy to use my affiliate link, use https://wp-unboxed.com/PT .

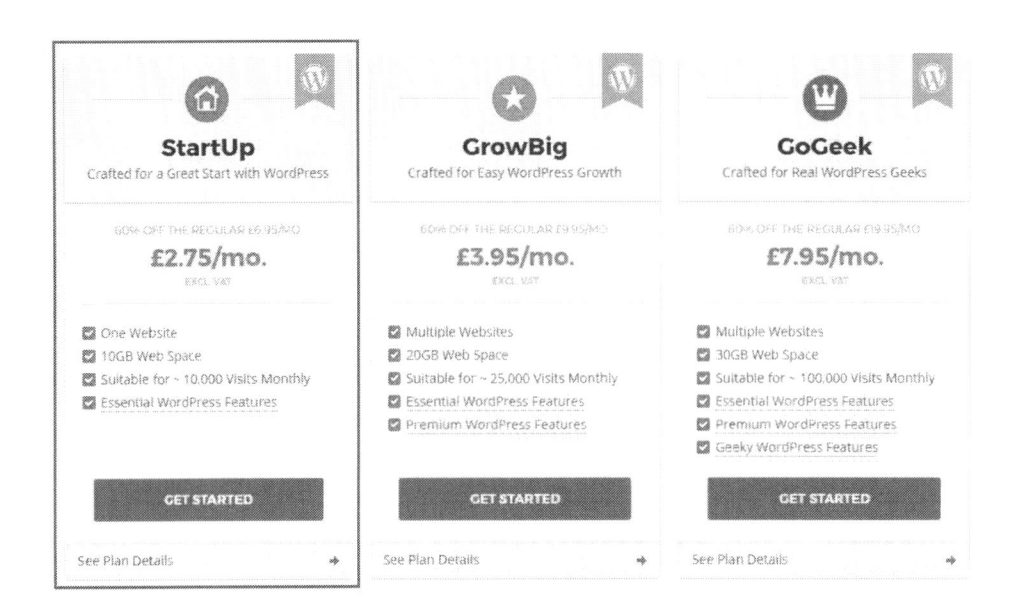

If you wish to use my promotional link, that is https://paulteague.com/SG

You're now presented with three options; you need to select the simplest and cheapest of those which is the **StartUp Plan**.

One of the things that you need to get used to when working online is the inclusion of upsells.

These are extras and add-ons that you'll be offered at the point of purchase.

These are all fine, there's nothing wrong with them, but most of the time you don't need them – or they'll just confuse you when you're starting out.

So I'll just advise you to skip the upsells because they're not essential to you.

I would also recommend that you take the annual option as that works out cheaper in the longer term – 60% cheaper in the case of Siteground.

Choosing your domain name
This is where things start to get exciting again because we now get to choose our domain name.

This is our URL, the link that we will promote as part of our web business.

It will be something like:

- myname.com

- mybusiness.net

- mybooktitle.com

In Siteground, we get a number of options (see image on next page).

1 – Register a new domain (see my notes on next page)

2 – I already have a domain – this is where you may have bought a domain name already.

You either need to transfer it over to Siteground, or repoint the nameservers towards Siteground.

If that last sentence makes you cry 'What's he talking about?!' I suggest that you buy a new domain name and keep things simple.

Or, get in touch with Siteground support and ask for their assistance – their support is excellent.

Changing name servers is easy, but I'm not going to explain it here as it's not a topic for first time Wordpress users.

3 – This is where you enter your preferred domain name. Beware, the option that you want may be taken already; sometimes you have to get creative if your domain name has been snatched up already.

4 – This is where we get to select our .com, .net, .info options. Just click the drop-down menu to see what's available.

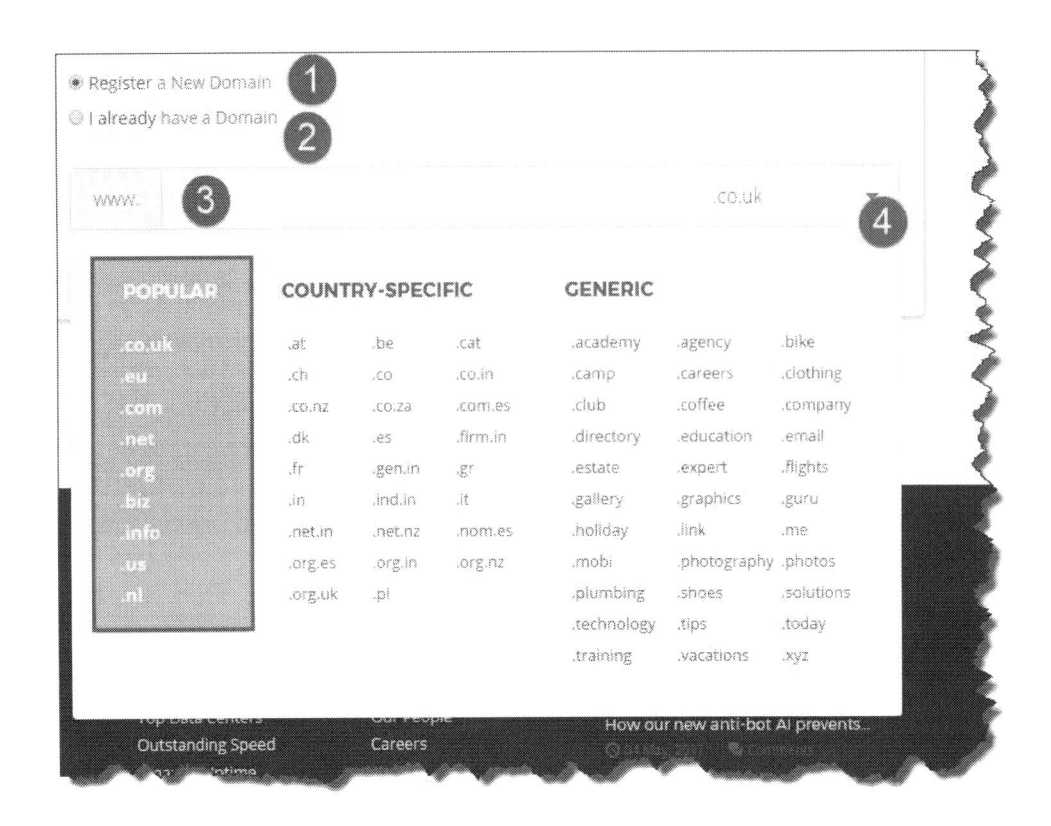

This is where you will see an immediate advantage over going for the free hosting option because now the world is our oyster when it comes to getting a domain name that really reflects our business.

Before you commit to a domain name, here are some points to note:

1 – All domain names are lower case, no spaces.

2 – These days you can use www or skip it altogether.

In my opinion, www is old school.

Rather than expressing my own blog link as https://www.paulteague.com, I just say 'Paul Teague.com' or write it as PaulTeague.com.

It works with or without the www, by the way. Many people still don't realise that.

However, be consistent with which format you use.

This is called **canonicalization**, and I'm not going to get into it in any detail in this book.

To keep it simple, use www or don't - just be consistent across the board.

3 – Make it easy to say and type.

21

4 – Avoid double letter clashes which make your URL hard to read, such as 'ee' next to each other, it doesn't really work in a URL.

An example of that is:

fineexpress.net

It just doesn't work when you read the URL. You have to sit, stare and figure it out.

A URL should be easy and straightforward.

5 – Keep it short.

We don't want to see thisismyridiculouslylongurl.com

It's too hard to read, and we'll give up typing it after 10 minutes.

6 – Use keywords!

This is great for Search Engine Optimization.

So if your name is the most important thing, use your name, e.g. paulteague.com

If the book title is the most important thing, use the title, e.g. thesecretbunker.net

If your product is the most important thing, use the product title in the domain name, i.e., ourwidgets.com

7 – Target your area, if you are a bricks and mortar or local service.

So rather than expresspizza.com you might go for expresspizzalincoln.co.uk.

8 – Watch out for rude, offensive or just plain funny word combinations.

There are some hilarious ones out there, just do a Google search for **funny domain names** if you don't believe me.

Make sure that your domain name isn't added to one of those lists.

9 – Avoid numbers and hyphens, particularly numbers.

Hyphens can cause confusion because people get them mixed up for underscores, and they're not nice to say out loud.

10 – Try and opt for something memorable.

Imagine you are at a networking event, using word of mouth to spread the news about your business.

Will we remember your domain name by the time we get home?

Make it easy for us to recall and check out online.

11 – Select the correct extension type.

.com and .net are generally the best options to use, in my opinion.

I settled for .net for my Secret Bunker trilogy (at thesecretbunker.net) because all of my favourite options had been taken already.

Sometimes you have to settle.

.info tends to be informational sites and .org is used for charities, non-profits, and voluntary organizations.

I'm never keen on .biz, just a personal preference. It never feels like the appropriate option to use for a classy, high-quality business.

So, in summary, get the .com if you can. If not opt for .net and if you still can't get what you want, you'll need to be creative.

I don't really like all of the new, fancy domain extensions that are available. In the end, we'll have to use them because all the best domain names will be gone.

In the meantime, hold out for the .com or .net of your choice.

12 – Make sure that you're not breaching somebody's copyright or trademark in your domain name.

If you do, there'll likely be some legal trouble waiting along the line.

Take legal advice if you're not sure about this and, if in doubt, the general rule of thumb on this point is 'don't risk it.'

Registering with Siteground

Now it's time to go through the Siteground registration process.

It's straightforward, but there are a few things along the way that I need point out to you.

Having worked through the previous pointers on domain name selection, you now need to find out if your domain name is available.

Enter your preferred domain name in the appropriate area and make sure that you have the correct .com or .net ending selected in the drop-down menu area.

You'll then get a message to let you know if your first choice of domain name is available (see 1 on the next page).

If the name you want is not available, this can be disappointing – and frustrating – but Siteground will suggest plenty of 'lookalike' domain names (see 2 on the next page) to assist you in narrowing down your choice:

The important thing to note about your domain name is that you renew it once a year, so the price you see displayed is the *annual* fee.

If you use my promotional link, you'll get a discount if you buy a new domain name.

The other thing to note is that Siteground is definitely not the cheapest place to buy your domain name, but if you want to avoid technical barriers to getting your site set up and live, it really is simplest to keep your domain name and hosting in the same place.

If you ever run a web business at any scale, my advice on this matter would be different, but for novice Wordpress users who just want a single website, this is the easiest course of action.

Next, you need to come up with a Username and Password to access your account.

Make it secure and consider becoming acquainted with https://www.lastpass.com/ in the longer term as it will help you considerably in making your website access much more secure.

The panel below is self-explanatory – just make that password a good one!

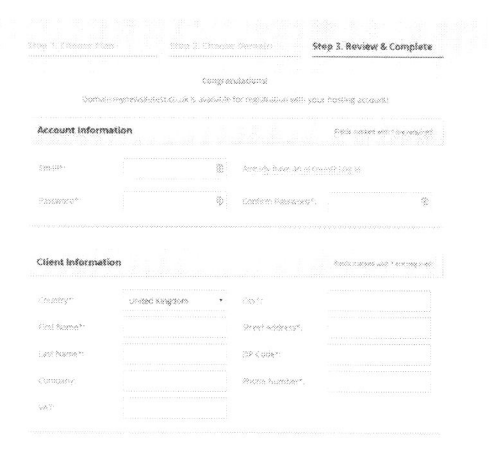

As you scroll down, you'll need to enter your payment information.

Remember to buy 12 months at a time because it's cheaper, and you don't need that SG Site Scanner addon-on, you can survive without it:

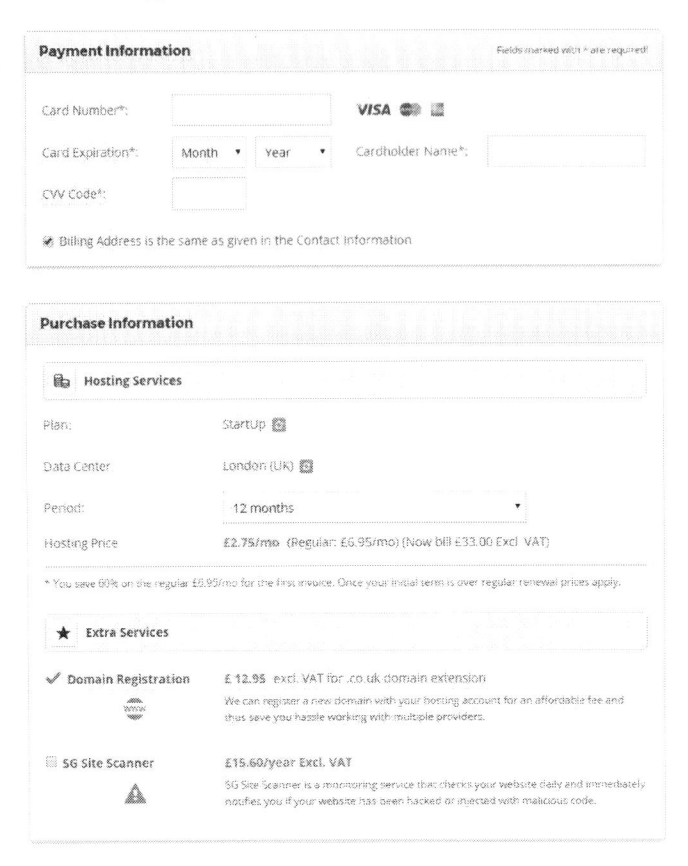

Next comes the nasty bit - having to pay - but this is really very good value by the time we've applied our discounts, so enter your payment details and just consider it a small but very necessary cost of doing business.

Remember, you could be running a shop. Your expenses would be a lot higher if you were.

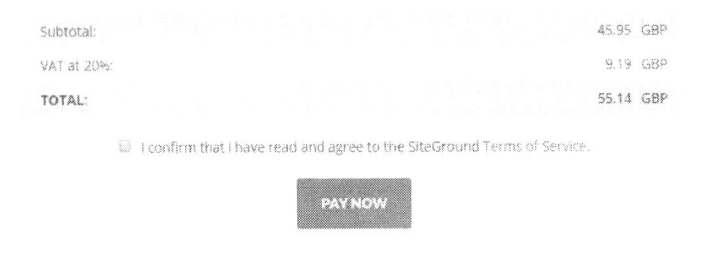

Take a moment to check out the terms and conditions. There's nothing horrible in there if you plan to run an above board and legitimate business, but you should always acquaint yourself with your responsibilities.

Once you have checked the terms and conditions, click that blue **Pay Now** button and you're on your way.

Siteground will now send you an email containing all of your information, and it will look like the example below:

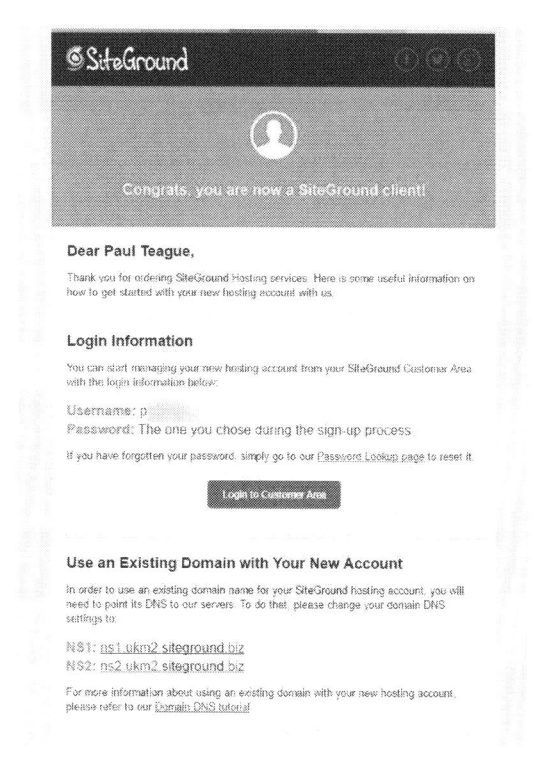

Click that orange **Login to Customer Area** on your welcome email and enter your details into the login panel, shown below:

Your Siteground work area looks like this – you need to click on **My Accounts**:

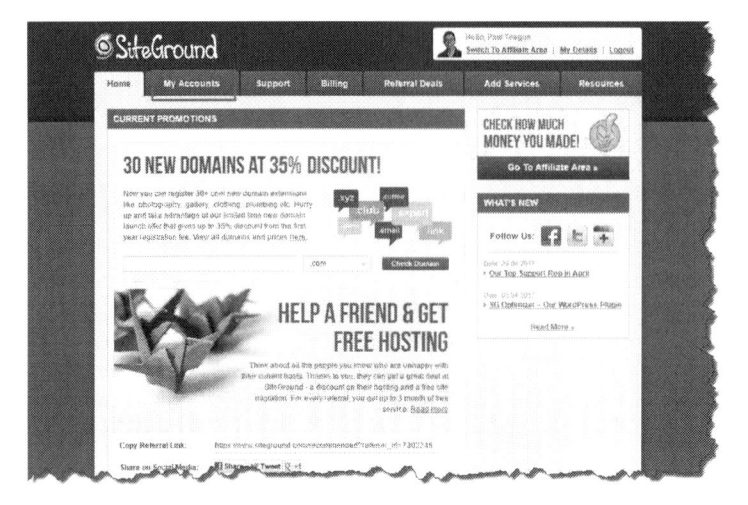

You will need to click on **Manage Account** next:

After that, we head for cPanel via that orange button marked **Go to cPanel**:

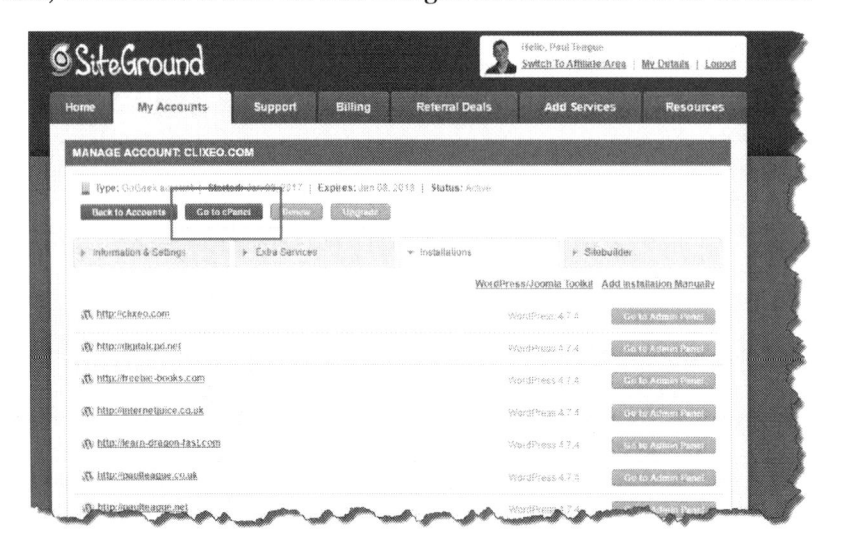

Remember, cPanel is just short for Control Panel.

You're then taken to the place where all the magic happens:

I know that the cPanel area can look overwhelming, but we only need to use a small part of it.

We're now ready to install your Wordpress site, and that simple process is going to take about 5 minutes maximum.

Installing Wordpress

This process is virtually identical on any web service which offers web hosting with cPanel which is why I recommend you always opt for cPanel even if you don't use Siteground.

It just makes life easy.

I've seen some people using horribly over-complicated web hosts, and I just think 'Why?' when life can be so easy with cPanel.

So, get ready to see a Wordpress site created with great ease in front of your own eyes.

Warning: When you register a new domain name it can take a little time to 'resolve.'

That means that you may buy the domain name and set up your website, but still be seeing a message like 'This site is awaiting completion' or some similar holding message.

Without wishing to overwhelm you with too much 'science' and have you shout 'Too much information!' at this book, I want to keep this simple.

Domain name resolution is a normal if frustrating process.

In the old days of the web, it used to take ages. Nowadays it seems to be quite fast.

However, it is not unheard of to have to wait 1-2 days for a domain name to work correctly.

The main point about this is not to panic.

If, after 2 days, you still have the default message showing, contact the Siteground or web host's helpdesk and ask for their advice or assistance.

The advantage of buying your domain name directly from your web host is that it usually speeds that process up considerably and I have known the resolving process to take very little time in many cases.

With that bit of information now out of the way, let's move on to the exciting stuff.

Step 1: In cPanel, head for AutoInstallers (1, below) and click on Wordpress (2, below).

Step 2: This takes us to the Wordpress area in Softaculous which, you may recall, I mentioned earlier in this book.

Click that blue **Install** button:

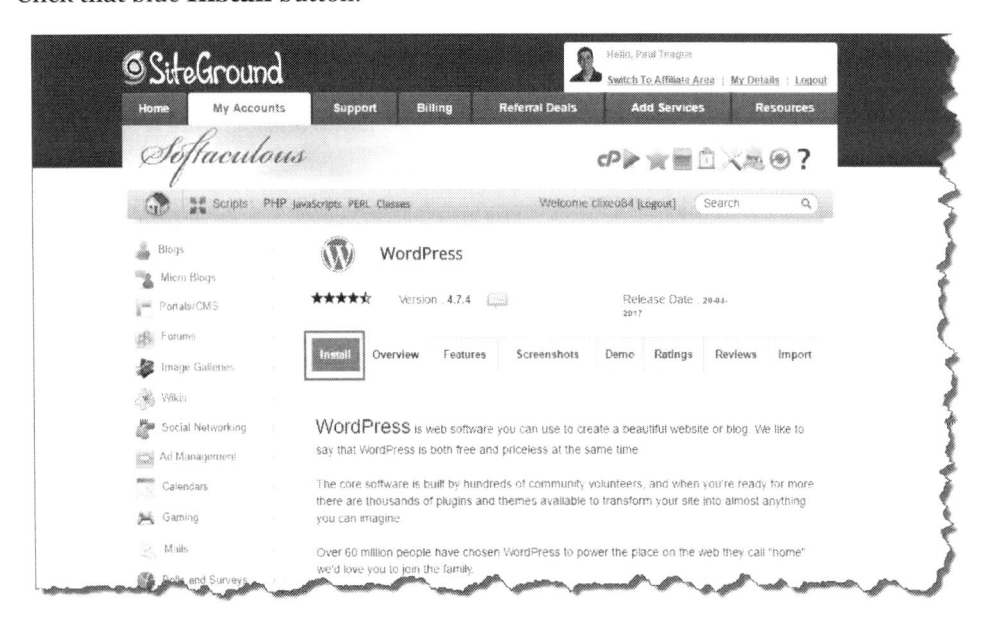

Step 3: At this stage, you are taken to a **Software Setup** screen, as shown below:

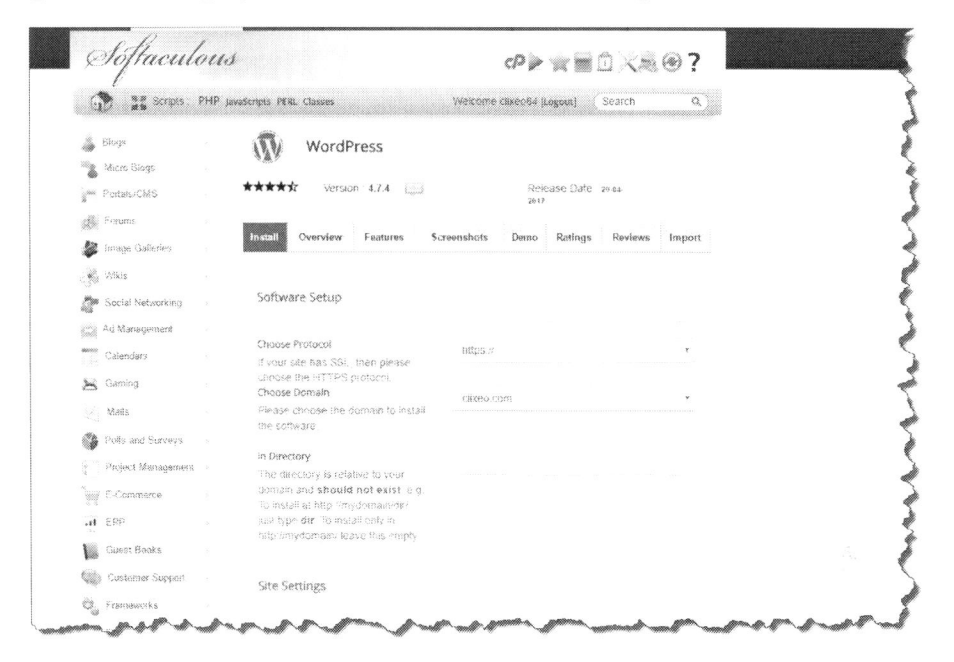

As you only have one domain name on this hosting account, life is simple.

Just leave all of those options (Choose Protocol/Choose Domain/In Directory) exactly as they are.

Scroll down the page to work through the other fields which need to be completed:

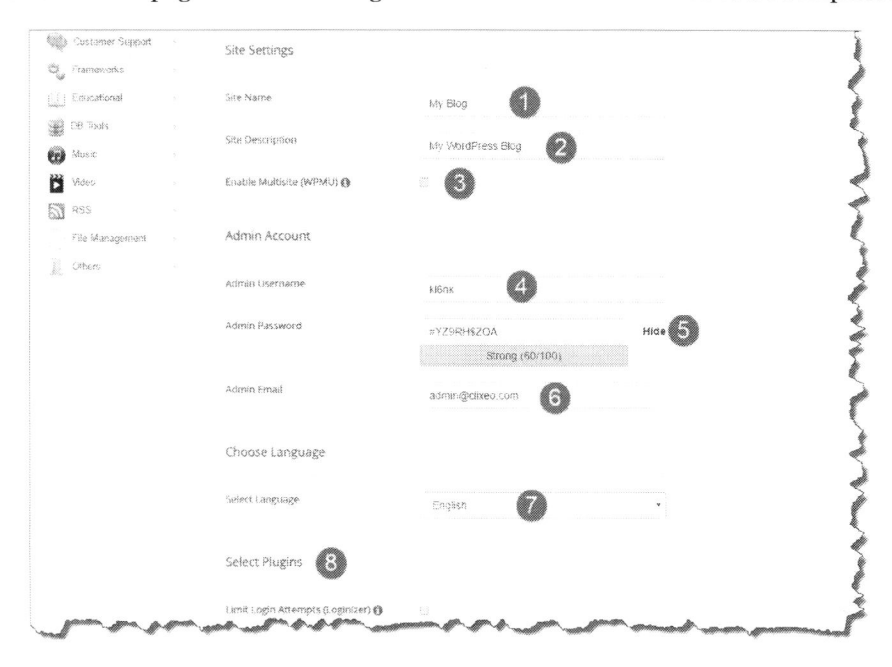

30

Now work through the following guidance for completing the Wordpress set-up process:

Install Wordpress

1: Site name – whatever you want to call this website or blog.

This will appear at the top of your Wordpress blog.

You can change this info later if you want to.

My site name is PaulTeague.com; my trilogy site name is The Secret Bunker.

Make it something short and descriptive.

2: Site Description – once again, you can change this later if you want to.

Just enter a simple tagline explaining what the site is all about.

3: Enable Multisite – ignore!

4: Admin Username – Don't use something obvious like 'admin'!

5: Admin Password: Softaculous will generate a lovely secure password for you and email your information to you as soon as your installation is finished.

Once again, I'd advise using a tool like https://www.lastpass.com/ to be as sure as you can that your security is good.

6: Admin Email – your blog login info will be sent to this email address.

Make sure it's an email address that you can easily access. You'll thank me later if you lose your password.

7: Select Language – Self-explanatory!

8: Select Plugins – For simplicity, leave all unchecked.

Finally, scroll down a little further to access the last options:

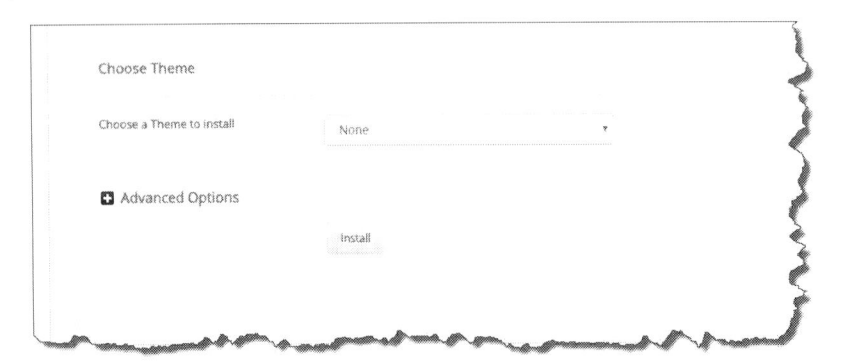

Leave **Choose a Theme to install** on None and ignore **Advanced Options**, as shown in the image on the previous page.

Just click on the **Install button** to complete the process, and you'll see the installation success message on your screen:

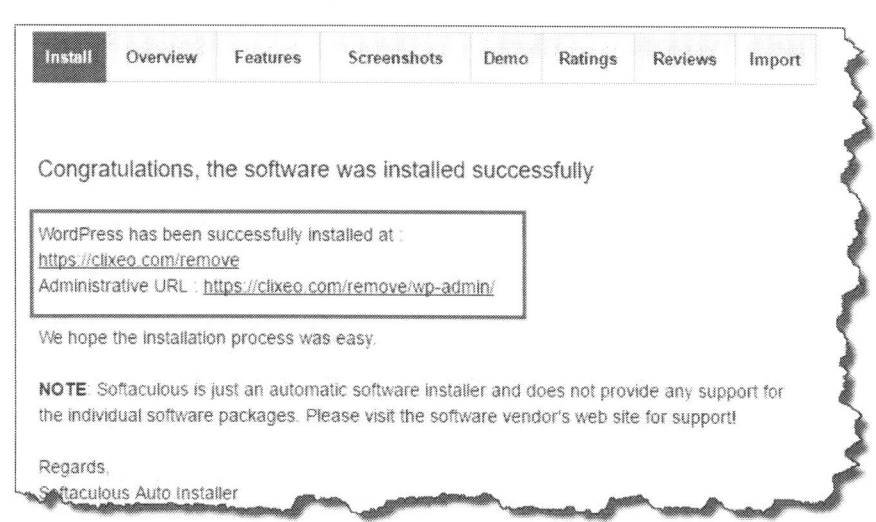

> Congratulations, the software was installed successfully
>
> WordPress has been successfully installed at:
> https://clixeo.com/remove
> Administrative URL: https://clixeo.com/remove/wp-admin/
>
> We hope the installation process was easy.
>
> **NOTE**: Softaculous is just an automatic software installer and does not provide any support for the individual software packages. Please visit the software vendor's web site for support!
>
> Regards,
> Softaculous Auto Installer

This is a copy of the email that you are sent to confirm your Wordpress installation:

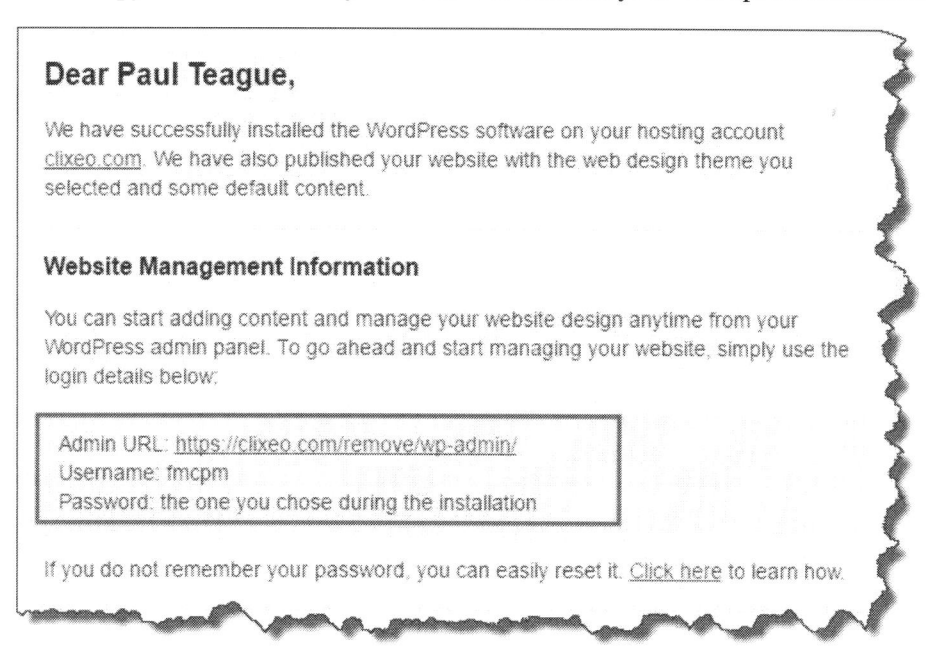

> **Dear Paul Teague,**
>
> We have successfully installed the WordPress software on your hosting account clixeo.com. We have also published your website with the web design theme you selected and some default content.
>
> **Website Management Information**
>
> You can start adding content and manage your website design anytime from your WordPress admin panel. To go ahead and start managing your website, simply use the login details below:
>
> Admin URL: https://clixeo.com/remove/wp-admin/
> Username: fmcpm
> Password: the one you chose during the installation
>
> If you do not remember your password, you can easily reset it. Click here to learn how.

You can click on Blogs and Wordpress in the Softaculous menu at any time to access your Wordpress installation:

For each installation you can easily access (see image below):

1: The **Clone** button (copy your site)

2: The **Site Backup** button

3: The **Edit** button

4: The **Uninstal**l button (to delete your Wordpress site)

This is what that interface looks like with several Wordpress sites installed.

You would only ever see it like this if you'd opted for Siteground's GrowBig or GoGeek services:

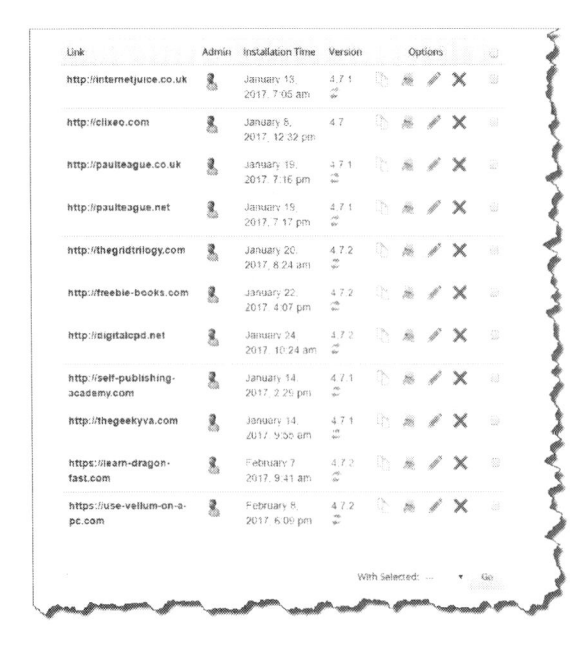

You now have a Wordpress blog.

It's as easy as that!

If you're lucky, your Wordpress site will already be available via your main domain name URL, but remember that it may take some time for you to be able to see your new Wordpress installation online. Give it up to 48 hours before you contact the Helpdesk at your hosting service.

Your main site will look something like this (current at the time of writing, this can vary depending on the default template installed at the time):

This brings us to the point that we reached with the free Hostinger example, shown earlier in this book.

Both basic installations are ugly at the moment but don't worry; we'll soon sort that out!

The **Hello world!** post is just a standard Wordpress thing; they always set up an initial post to get you underway.

With Siteground, they add in some generic articles to populate the site.

We'll delete all of this 'holding' content later.

Finally, you can log in to your admin area via the **Login** button in the blog menu, towards the bottom right-hand side of the homepage.

Don't worry if you can't find it, the format of the Wordpress login page is always the same.

If your URL is http://myblog.com, your admin area login will be http://myblog.com/wp-login.php.

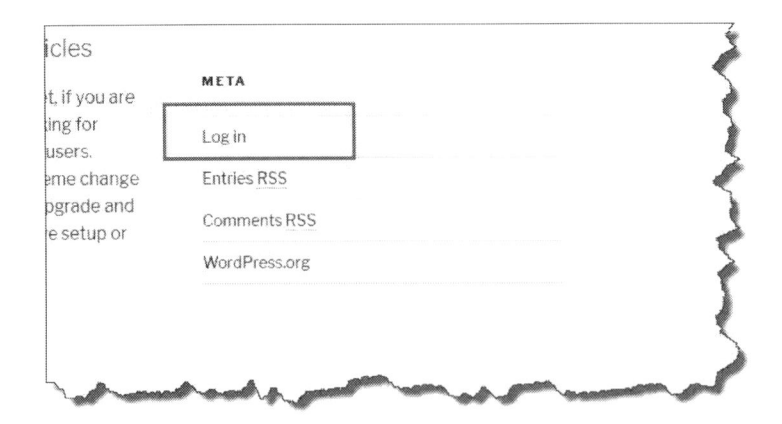

Alternatively, use the admin URL in your **WordPress Installation Confirmation** email.

It's the link that ends with /wp-admin/

Both options will take you to this Wordpress login area:

Note that you can reset your password using the **Lost your password?** link at the bottom of the login form.

Once you have logged in, you will be taken to the Wordpress dashboard.

This is where all the blogging magic happens.

We are now at exactly the same stage as we left off in the earlier free installation guide, so the next chapter will talk you through this dashboard and show you the most important areas.

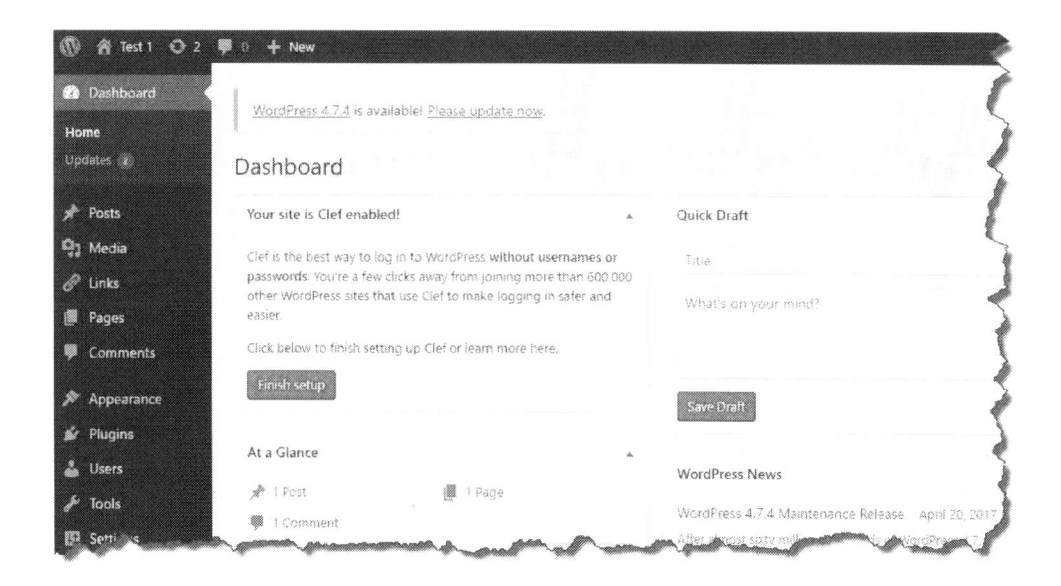

Just a quick note about Wordpress menus before we move on.

You'll notice a Wordpress logo right in the top left-hand corner of the menu area; this just gives access to some Wordpress 'extras' such as the Support Forums and Documentation:

I can't recall ever using this; I just head for the main admin menu which is indicated by the small house icon ith the name of my blog to the right-hand side of it.

Chapter 4: Getting to Know the Wordpress Dashboard

At this stage you should now have the following:

1 – A free or paid for Wordpress blog.

2 – Access to your Wordpress admin area (also referred to as the Dashboard).

From this point onwards, it doesn't matter if you use free hosting or paid for hosting because everything is exactly the same.

You get the same Wordpress software, and everything is in the same place.

Do You Need an Upgrade?

Depending on which hosting service that you used to install your Wordpress site, you may need to run an update straight away.

Wordpress updates are a regular part of life, and you should always run the update as soon as it is offered to you.

Often updates contain essential security patches. At other times, it's a load of cool new features.

Whatever it is, always keep your site up-to-date.

Wordpress will notify you in your Dashboard when an update is available:

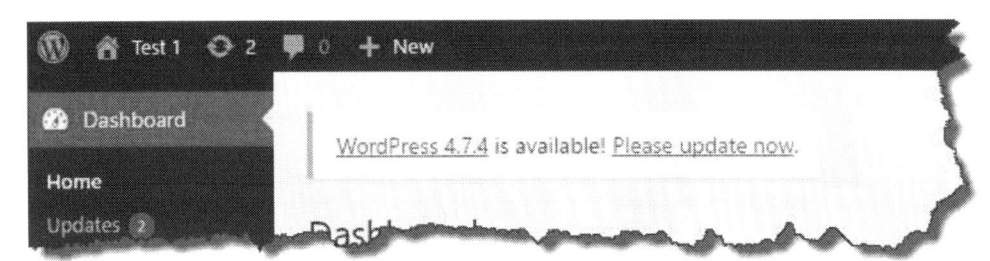

Just click on the **Please update now** link, and you'll be taken to a new page.

Don't be phased by the information in this new area. Just click the button marked **Update Automatically,** and Wordpress will take care of everything for you.

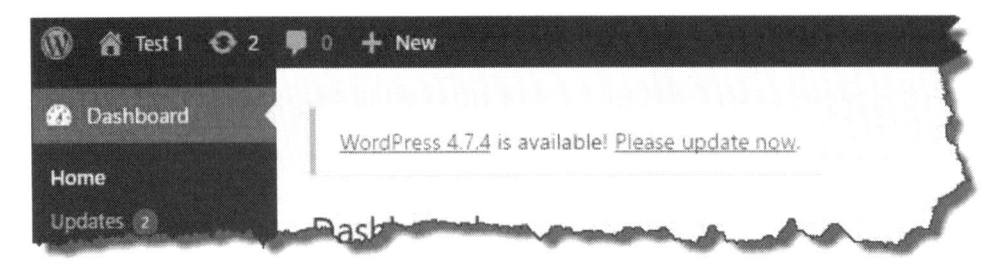

Note: Wordpress always adds an advisory note about backing up your database and files.

This is always good practice, but the aim of this book is to get you started as soon as possible.

We don't actually have any blog content to lose just yet!

So once again, rather than overwhelm you with new things to learn, I want to focus only on the most essential things here. I'll recommend a free backup plugin later.

To put it in context, I *never* backup prior to installing a routine update (I know, I know, one of these days I'll regret it!) but I do backup my sites elsewhere, so I know that I can restore them if need be.

This is something for me to cover if I ever write a book 2. However, it's most important to get you started, first of all. That way you'll get the impetus and enthusiasm to learn more of the housekeeping chores.

Once you have clicked that **Update Automatically** button, Wordpress will perform the upgrade.

You'll see a message telling you that the update is in progress. For trouble free operation, don't interrupt this process or close your browser until it finishes.

Also, don't panic if you see this message:

> Briefly unavailable for scheduled maintenance. Check back in a minute.

Give it a moment, and your website will be back.

After the update, you'll be asked to log in once again.

The login form may have adopted a slightly different appearance. That's because it too may have been updated.

Log in with your usual Wordpress credentials and head back to your dashboard.

Please remember that we just updated Wordpress and it may have changed appearance slightly.

It's a bit like Dr. Who; it's the same person underneath all the time, it's just a different look.

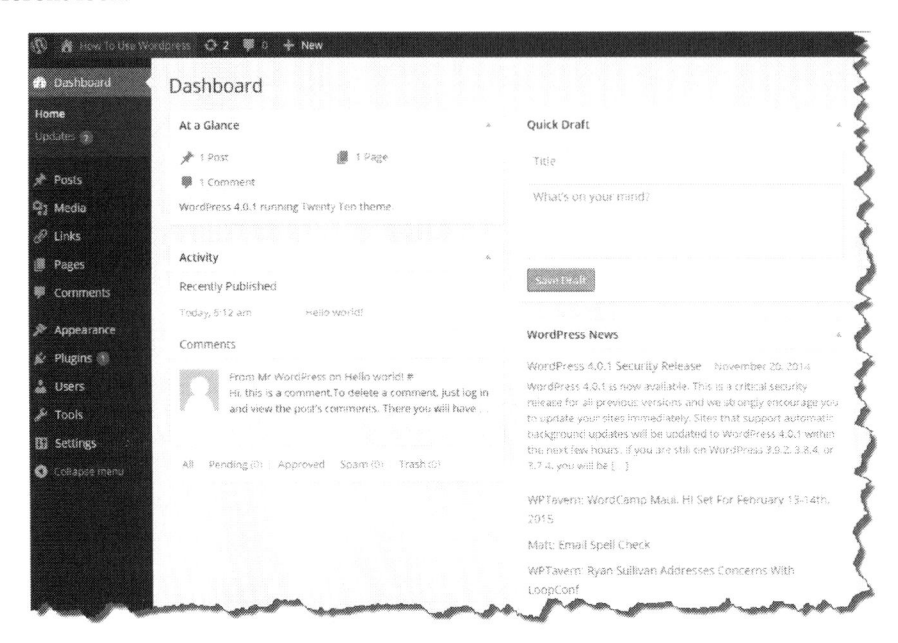

One thing that I can reassure you about however is that I have been using Wordpress for many years now and updates are never so massive that I haven't got a clue what's going on.

The basic furniture and orientations are always the same. It may look a little different, but most things are still where you found them prior to the update.

Dashboard Basics

For the time being, if you have an alert indicating that any other updates are due, please ignore them. We'll get to them later as we explore the dashboard further.

I'll be very honest with you. As an established user, I don't even look at the large area with the light grey background which takes up the majority of this space, I work almost exclusively via the menus on the left-hand side.

I recommend that you do the same. Move your attention away from the distractions, focus on the stuff that matters.

So let's take a close look at the main Wordpress menu:

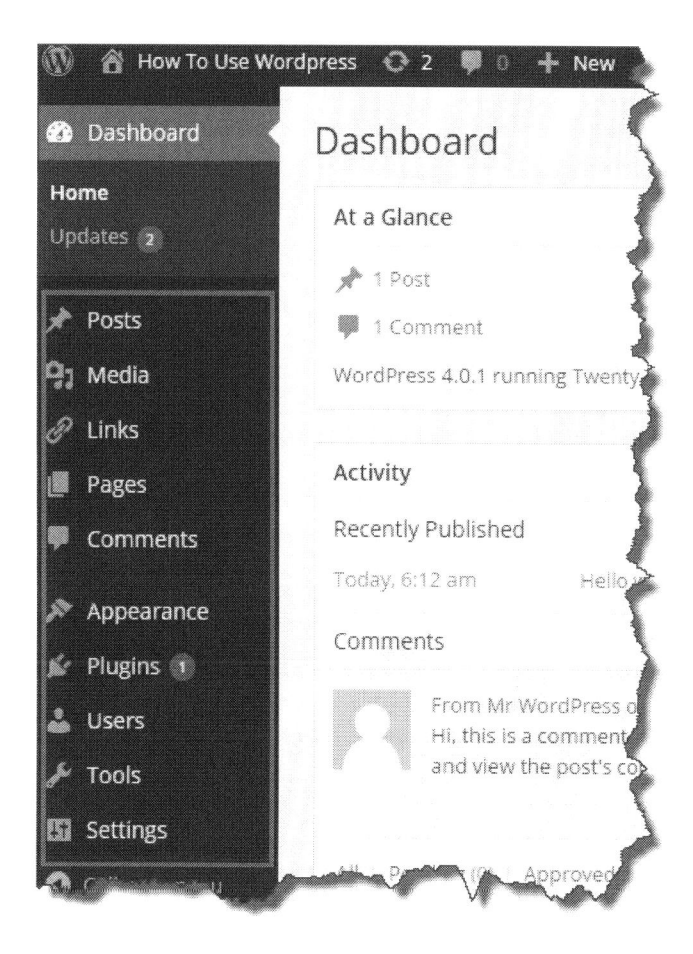

Here's a quick guide to what everything does. We'll need to dig deeper as we move along:

Posts – This is where you create, edit and delete your blog posts.

Media – This is where you upload, edit, and delete (mainly) images.

Wordpress will actually let you upload many common file types here, including some video files, but you are limited by the *size* of the file.

I use it mostly for images and .pdf reports.

Videos are always best placed on YouTube or a similar video service in the first instance.

Links – I haven't really used this for some time, to be honest with you, but it is pretty handy for the first-time blogger.

Wordpress allows you to create a **Blogroll,** which is, very simply, a list of links to your favourite websites.

The reason I don't use this nowadays is that I want readers to stay on my blog – not go somewhere else – and if they do go somewhere else, I want it to be an affiliate product or another one of my own sites.

My blog is there to generate income. However, if you don't care about that, by all means, create a Blogroll.

Wordpress adds several links of its own to get you started; you may well want to delete these, though.

Pages – Pages are different to Posts.

Remember right at the beginning of this book I talked about the difference between static websites and blogs?

Well, in very simple terms, pages are where all that static information goes.

It's the 'About Us' and 'Contact Us' sort of material - pages which you set up once and seldom change.

I also use pages for 'Privacy Info,' 'Terms and Conditions' and 'Disclosure' sections.

Posts are where the creative content goes.

Comments – One of the cool things about Wordpress, and blogs in general, is in the ability of readers to interact.

It's one of the big differences between those old fashioned static websites and the newer blogging platforms.

However, comments can be a bit of a curse on Wordpress too; you'll soon tire of comment spam.

But don't worry, there's a solution for that. We'll talk about it later in the plugins chapters.

Appearance – This is a really important section, in fact, it gets its own chapter because it's so important.

This is where you control how your blog looks in terms of headers, backgrounds, content and menus.

It's really easy to use, but it does require some knowledge of the basics.

Plugins   This is the powerhouse of Wordpress. Plugins are amazing things which allow you to add incredible functionality to your blog.

This topic has a chapter of its own. In fact, it gets two chapters in all - that's how important it is.

More on plugins later.

Users – Depending on how you choose to set up your blog, you may wish to have readers registering on your Wordpress site.

This is where you can administrate your site users.

Most users will just be readers of your content and, once again, this is not an area that I spend a lot of time in.

For the purposes of this introductory guide to Wordpress, the key point to make is that the **Users** area is where you can administrate and update *your own* Wordpress account.

Tools – Once again, this is an extremely useful area, but not something that we need to go into detail about in this book.

In simple terms, this is where you can **Export** all of your blog posts if you want to move them to a different software platform – or perform a *simple* backup of your content.

The **Import** function is equally useful if you are bringing in content from, say, a Blogger site.

There are a number of different uses for **Import,** but I won't cover them in this guide, which focuses only on new installations of Wordpress.

However, this area gets more powerful by the year, and you can now transfer many popular types of blog format into a Wordpress site.

42

Settings – This is another crucial area of Wordpress and one which will also be allocated its own chapter.

There's some really important stuff in here, and it's where you should always head first of all when you set up a new Wordpress blog, even before you start to create content.

It's here that we'll head in the next chapter.

Chapter 5: Wordpress Settings

Whenever I have set up a new Wordpress installation, there is always a set of jobs which I do before I move onto things like themes and plugins.

The reason for this is that they're all very important so, to make sure that I don't forget them, I work through them first.

They're all extremely easy, and I'll explain why I do them as we go along.

Step 1: Remove the Default Post

Wordpress installs a demonstration post by default.

That's fine the first time you use it, but it gets a bit wearing if you install it regularly!

We need to delete it as it's not required.

We could leave it there of course, but we might as well start as we mean to go on, keeping a tidy blog.

So, first of all, navigate to posts via the left-hand menu.

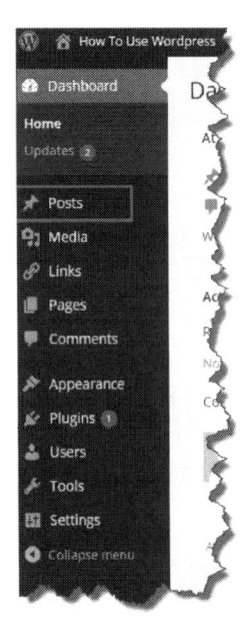

Next, we need to click on the checkbox next to the **Hello World!** post (marked 1 in the image below) and then click the **Bulk Actions** drop-down menu (marked 2 in the image below).

In a Siteground installation, you'll have the following post to delete:

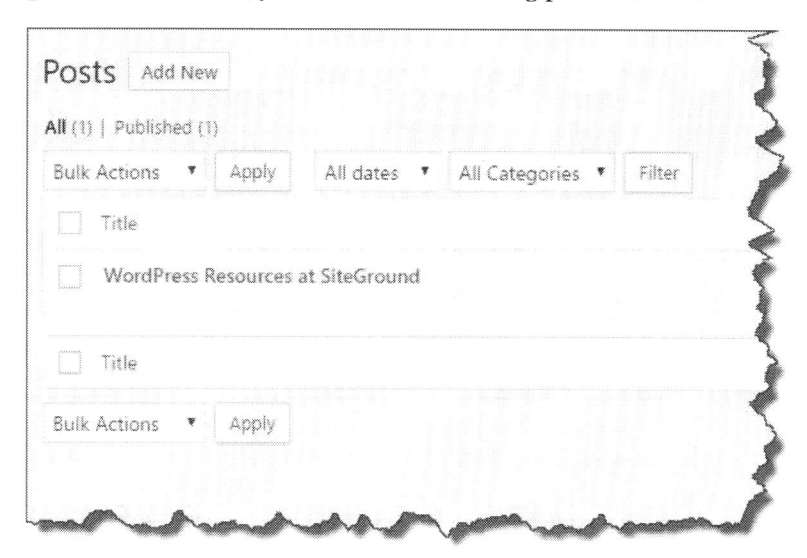

Just tick the box of any posts that you want to remove.

In the Bulk Actions drop-down menu, you need to select **Move to Trash** then **Apply** to complete the action.

44

The good news about this is that, if you deleted in error, you could undo this action:

Your post sits in a Trash area unless you decide to permanently delete it, so it can always be retrieved if you later regret your actions.

Step 2: Remove the Default Links.

Unless you're particularly keen to keep these, I always remove them.

Click on **Links** in the left-hand menu.

You can automatically select all of the links at one time by checking the box **Name**, which will place ticks next to all of the links (1 in the image below).

Next click on **Bulk Actions** (2 in the image above), select **Delete** and then **Apply.**

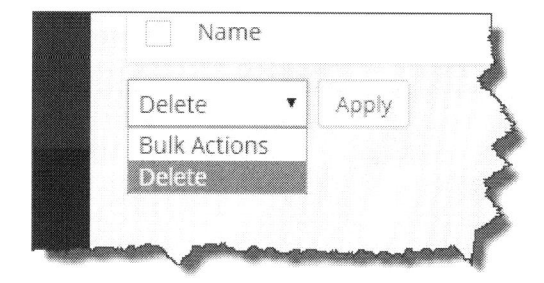

This will remove all of those links.

Step 3: Remove the Default Comment.
Wordpress adds a demonstration comment just to show new users what they look like.

It's good housekeeping to remove this at the beginning.

Once again, it's very easily done, and these routine activities will quickly familiarize you with the straightforward process of deleting content in Wordpress.

Start by clicking on **Comments** in the left-hand menu.

46

Click on the checkbox next to the comment from 'Mr. Wordpress' as shown by 1 in the image below (yes, there's even room for humour when you use Wordpress!), then head for the drop-down menu (indicated by 2 in the image below).

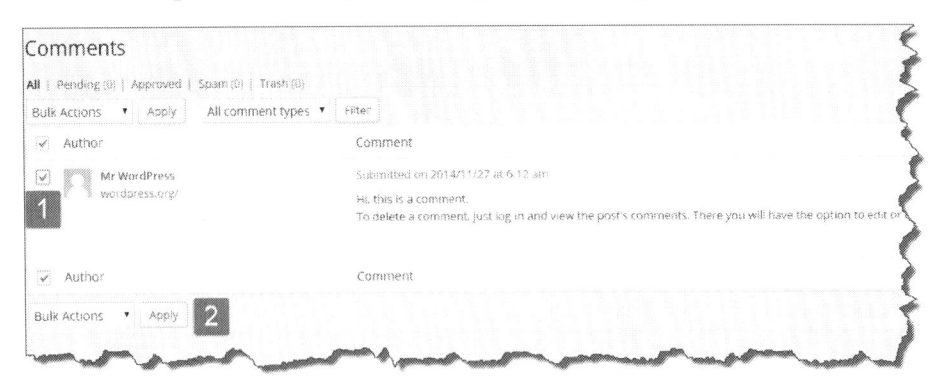

In Siteground, the comment looks a little different, but delete it in exactly the same way:

47

Click on **Bulk Actions**, select **Move To Trash**, then click on **Apply**.

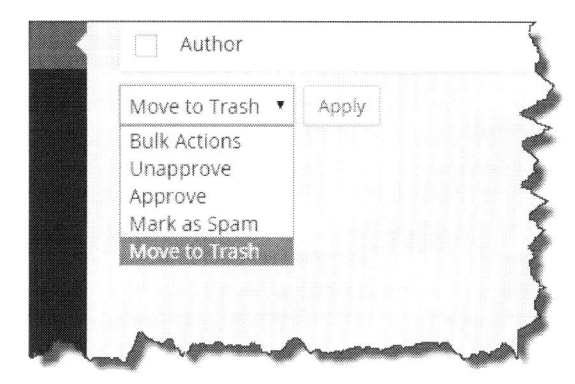

You'll note that we use **Move To Trash** rather than **Delete** at this point.

This enables us to undo the deletion if we make it in error, or if we change our minds afterwards.

Step 4: Remove the Default Page

Wordpress gives you a default page in addition to a post. Once again, we don't need it, so we'll delete it.

To do that, firstly, navigate to **Pages** in the left-hand menu:

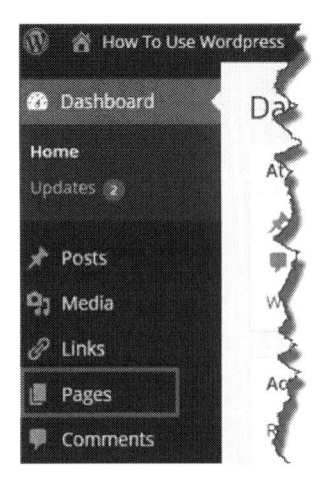

Just as we did with our unwanted post earlier, check the box next to **Sample Page** and then click on the **Bulk Actions** drop-down menu.

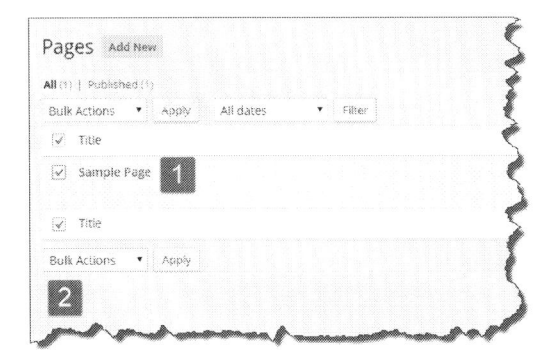

In Siteground, you may find that there aren't any default pages.

If that's the case, and there's nothing to delete, feel free to move on.

In the drop-down menu, select **Move to Trash** then **Apply**.

This deletes the unwanted page.

As with posts, if you delete a page in error, it can be retrieved from the Trash unless you go on to delete it permanently:

1 page moved to the Trash. Undo

Step 5: Remove an Unwanted Plugin.

Plugins are allocated two chapters later on in this book so for now we're just going to perform a very simple operation.

We're going to delete the **Hello Dolly** plugin, and any other plugins that are sitting in that area – the selection varies by hosting company.

So click on **Plugins** in the left-hand menu to begin this operation:

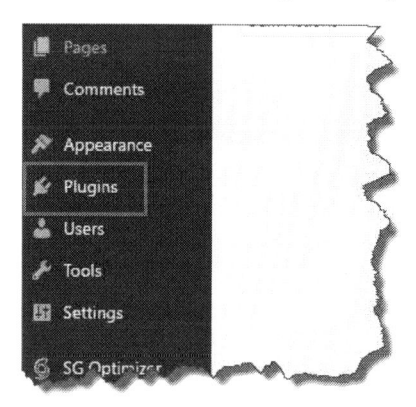

In Siteground, and with other hosting companies, you may well see that Jetpack has been installed.

This is a great 'catch-all' plugin for those who are new to Wordpress, but we won't be using it:

This is the selection of pre-installed plugins that come with a Siteground installation at the time of writing.

is selection will vary from hosting company to hosting company.

It really doesn't matter; we're deleting the lot anyway.

Make sure each box is checked. Clicking the **Plugin** checkbox on the top left-hand side will check each of the boxes, rather than you having to go through them individually:

You could just click on the **Delete** link under each plugin and remove them one by one:

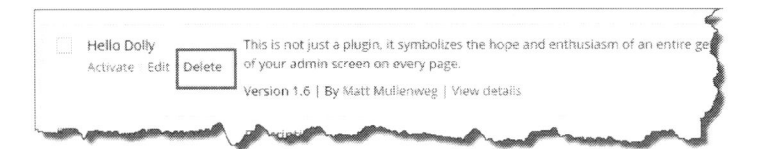

Also, you will not be able to delete any plugin that is activated – just click **Deactivate** if required.

If you are removing multiple plugins (if you used the free Hostinger account you might want to remove Limit Login Attempts for instance), we will use the checkboxes and **Bulk Actions** drop-down menu.

Click the menu (1, below), select **Delete** and then click **Apply** (3):

51

We are now asked to confirm that deletion:

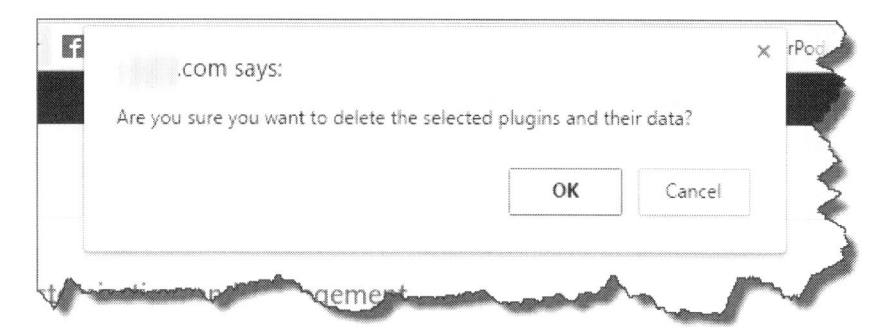

> .com says:
> Are you sure you want to delete the selected plugins and their data?
> OK   Cancel

This all looks a bit severe, but it's fine. Go ahead and click the button marked Yes, **Delete these files.**

That's it; we have now removed the unwanted plugin or plugins:

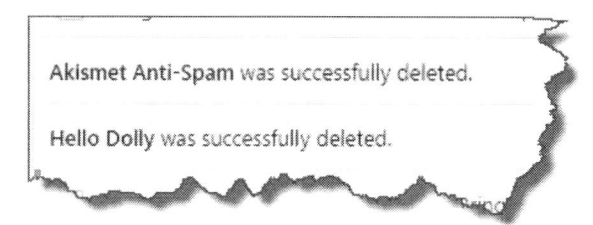

> Akismet Anti-Spam was successfully deleted.
>
> Hello Dolly was successfully deleted.

It's worth noting that once you delete a plugin, it's gone. You'd have to reinstall it if you'd made an error.

Having said that, Wordpress does generally retain the data.

So, if you created any links, fields or whatever it was that the plugin helped you to do, it'll usually still be there once you reinstall the plugin again.

You can just leave a plugin deactivated; you don't always have to delete it.

I use this simple guidance as my 'rule of thumb':

Will I ever use this plugin again?

Yes = Deactivate

No = Delete

I am using it already = Leave it alone

We'll be returning to plugins later.

52

Step 6: Adjust Some Essential Settings.

That Settings menu gives us direct access to six options – General, Writing, Reading, Discussion, Media, and Permalinks:

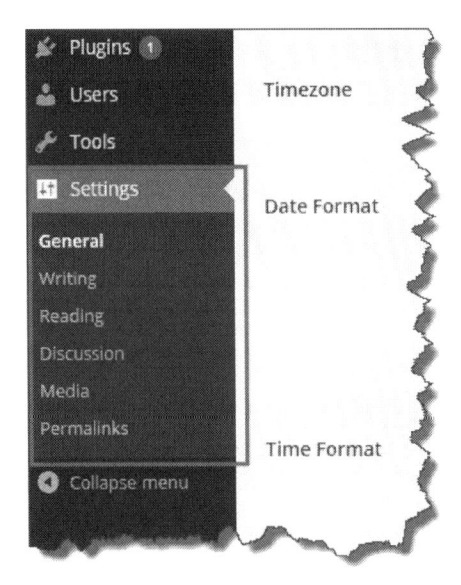

This is really quite important stuff; the previous 5 steps were about tidiness and good house-keeping, these next steps are really important for the wellbeing of your blog.

1: General

(See image below)

Change your **Site Title** and **Tagline** if you don't like what you used when you originally set up your blog.

Hopefully, you'll recall that we set these right at the beginning of the installation process.

Remember, you can change these at any time.

Your **Wordpress Address** and **Site Address** are filled automatically, so don't change them.

The email address is filled automatically. Only change it if there's a better one to use or if you change your email address.

You'll get Wordpress (essential) notifications via this email address so make sure that it's one that you can check easily and regularly.

Leave Membership as it is, for now, i.e., unchecked.

When you become more experienced with using Wordpress, you may wish to change this setting.

For now, I just want to show you how to set up a basic site, so we'll leave it at the default setting:

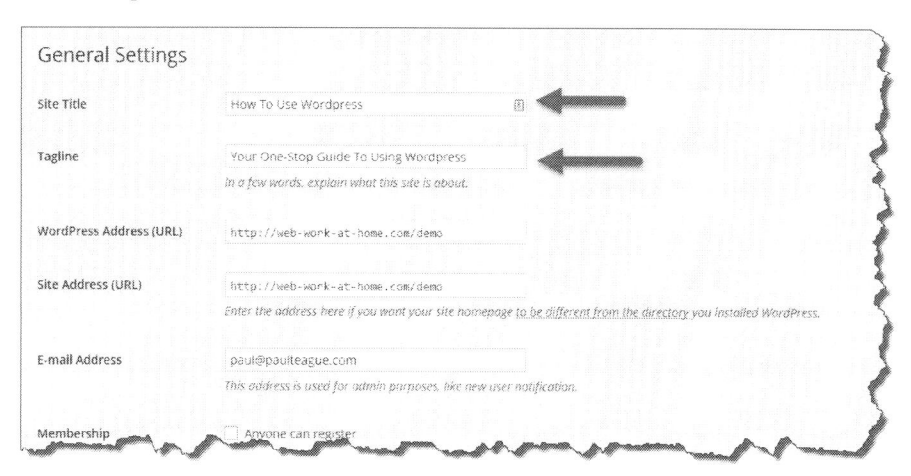

The lower settings are pre-defined. Change them to suit your own tastes and time preferences, but leave **New User Default Role** on **Subscriber**.

Remember to save any changes that you make by clicking the Save Changes button at the bottom of the page:

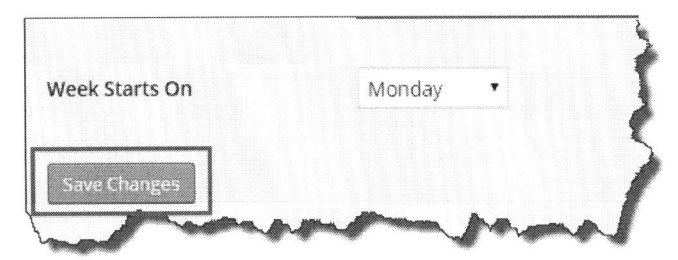

2: Writing

No need at present to change any of the default settings in the Writing section:

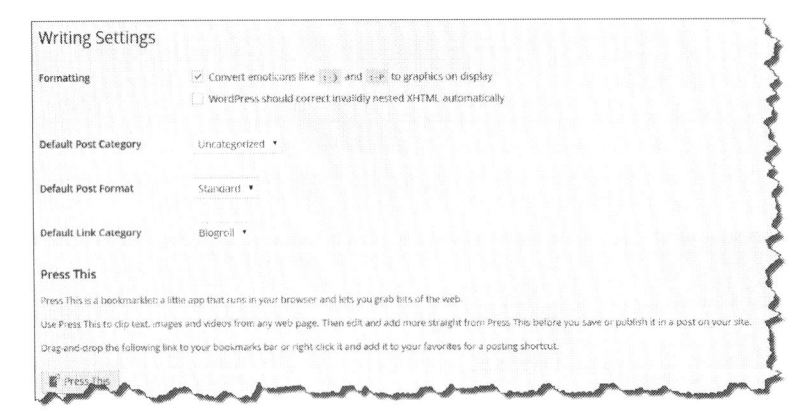

You may, later on, wish to set a new **Default Post Category** or **Default Link Category**, but until we take a closer look at categories and links, they can stay unchanged:

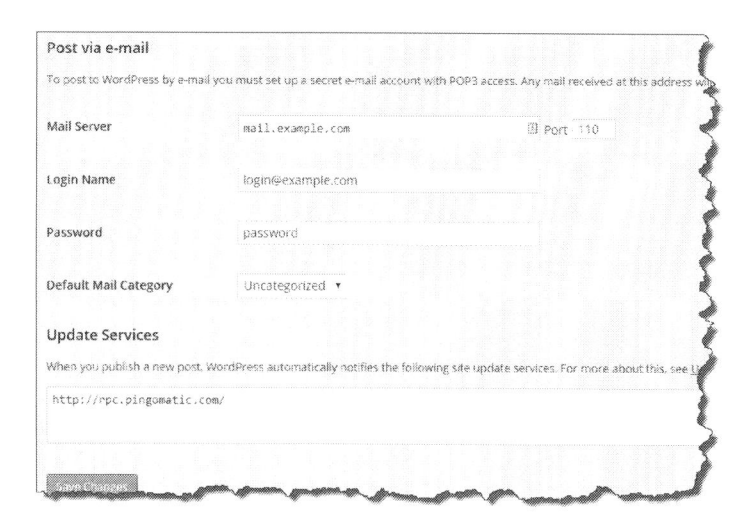

This is advanced stuff in the lower part of the page (see image above), leave it well alone for now.

3: Reading

Once again, no need to change anything here for the time being.

You must make sure that the Search Engine Visibility checkbox remains *unchecked* (this is the default) or else the search engines will not be able to find and index your blog.

That will mean that nobody can find your site.

The only time we'd ever check that box is if we were creating a private membership area or a blog that was not available to the public.

Everything else in that section can remain untouched; it won't bother you at all until you become a more advanced Wordpress user.

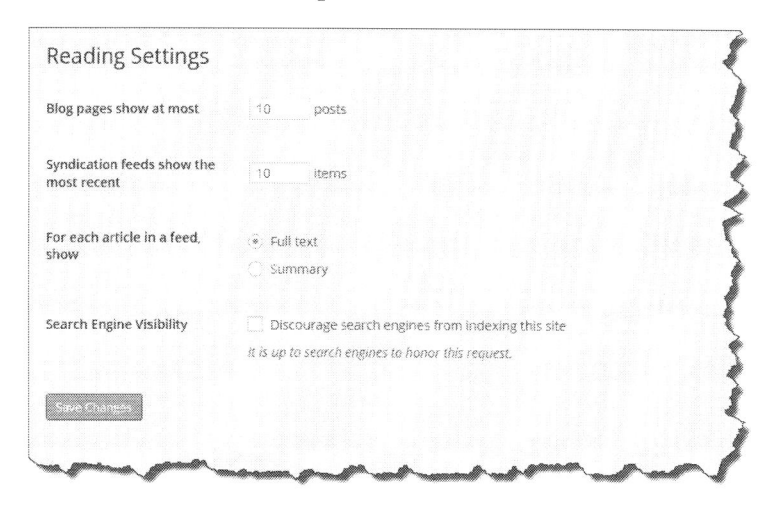

56

4: Discussion

I'd recommend leaving the discussion settings in the default settings in the first instance.

You'll get a feel for how it all works when you get your new website underway, and the comments and interactions begin.

For now, though, leave everything as it is.

I have been known to disable comments entirely at times – depending on the blog – or enhancing them with a very nice plugin called CommentLuv, which you can find at https://wordpress.org/plugins/commentluv/ if you're feeling ambitious later on.

You will get many spam comments on your Wordpress after a while.

They become a bit of an annoyance!

Akismet – which is installed by default – is a very effective tool in combating this problem.

However, for business websites, it is a paid-for plugin, I will substitute it with a free option later in the book.

Here are the **Comment Moderation** and **Comment Blacklist** settings:

The **Avatars** section is important, I think.

By default, if somebody comments on your blog you'll get a horrible, greyed out thumbnail image.

I hate those and would rather see the faces of real people wherever possible.

Many people use the Gravatar service at https://en.gravatar.com/ these days, and I'd recommend that you do the same.

Gravatar lets you use globally recognised avatars. Essentially, it hooks up with all of the email addresses that you use to login to sites.

It automatically pulls in your Gravatar image.

It looks good on your blog, and it looks good when you comment on somebody else's blog. Think of it as effective and consistent branding.

My recommendation is to use Gravatar on your blog and to sign up for the free service yourself at https://en.gravatar.com/.

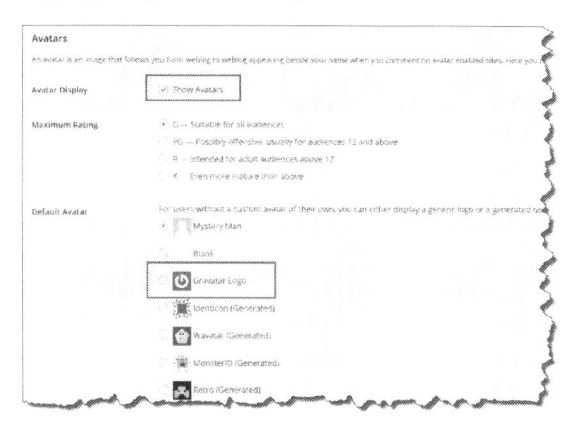

5: Media

When you start using Wordpress, there's no real need to change the **Media Setting**s defaults.

It's one of those things that you may find restrictive in the longer term, depending on what you are doing, but I don't think that in all my years using Wordpress I have ever touched those settings.

I do recommend that you leave **Organize my uploads into month and year based folders,** as that will become a really handy feature as your blog grows in size.

6: Permalinks

This is the really important setting; you must change this.

I'm really surprised that Wordpress hasn't set this by default, but it remains this way at the time of writing so you must always manually force it through.

Permalinks basically refer to the web links that will be generated when you create **Posts** and **Pages**.

The default format is horrible, and you must fix it!

My preferred post format is **Post name**.

There is a very good reason for this by the way and without wanting to get too geeky, with basic SEO principles, a nice, word-based URL which includes your keywords will always be preferred by Google.

Some people like to use **Month and name**, but most of us are unable to write posts that often and it can make your blog feel quickly dated, in my opinion.

So stick to **Post name,** and you're good to go.

Remember to click on **Save Changes** to confirm your setting.

Finally, we get to **Category base** and **Tag base**.

Routine users will not need to change these. I have never had to tweak this particular setting in any of the Wordpress installations that I have carried out.

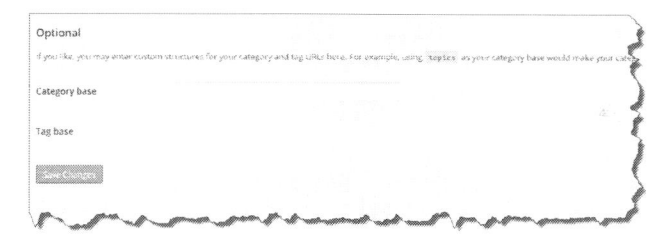

That's it for settings; your blog is all set up and ready to go.

We can now look at the creative activities, such as generating new content and adding functionality with cool plugins.

Chapter 6: Creating Posts and Pages

The Difference Between Pages and Posts

Wordpress itself gives an excellent explanation of the difference between pages and posts in the article at http://en.support.wordpress.com/post-vs-page/.

I will summarize it even more, though.

Pages are for static content, for information like 'About Us,' 'Where to find us,' 'Contact Us' and so on.

They are usually set up when you start your blog and seldom change thereafter.

Posts are for your *latest* content – articles, 'how to' guides, latest product release info and so on.

In addition, and this is really important on a blog, **Posts** are arranged in date order, i.e., the order that you created them.

If you think about it, that's a great thing because you always want your freshest content to display first.

There is no limit to the number of **Pages** or **Posts** that you can create.

Categories Explained

Before we create our first **Post**, you need to think about how your blog categories will be organized.

This is how Wordpress describes **Categories**:

'Categories provide a helpful way to group related posts together, and to quickly tell readers what a post is about. Categories also make it easier for people to find your content. Categories are similar to but broader than, tags.'

If you were writing a Social Media blog, your **Categories** might be:

Facebook

Twitter

LinkedIn

YouTube

To set up your categories, click on the **Posts** link in the left-hand menu.

This will give you access to **Categories**, as shown on the next page.

Uncategorized is the default category, Wordpress will insist on you using that category if you don't change it to something else.

Here's a Search Engine Optimization tip, though.

You should use Categories and Tags every time because it helps to signpost your content clearly in the search engines.

Never be lazy and leave everything in Uncategorized.

Not only is it a sign of a sloppy blog, but you will also do yourself a disservice in the long term because you will not be helping yourself in the search engines.

Step 1: To create a category, first give it a name.

This can be upper or lower case.

In my Social Media example, my categories would be:

Facebook

Twitter

LinkedIn

YouTube

Step 2: Next add the slugs, and note that these must be lower case.

In my Social Media example, my slugs would be:

facebook – twitter -linkedin - youtube

Step 3: I tend to keep my categories simple, so I don't use the hierarchy system.

Unless your blog is really complicated, I suggest that you always go for simple.

Step 4: The description doesn't show on most themes, but if you wish to add a keyword or two here, by all means, do so.

Click on Add New Category to create your new category.

Just repeat this process and add as many categories as you wish.

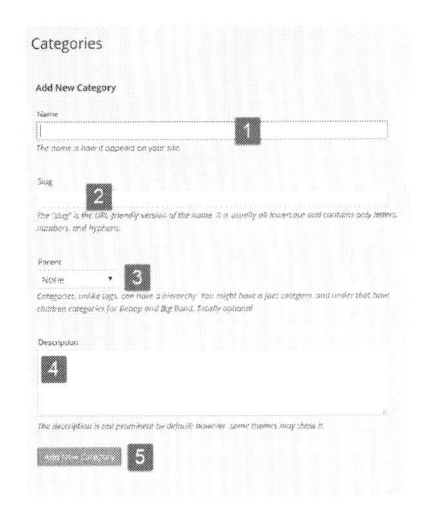

In my Social Media example, my Categories would look like this:

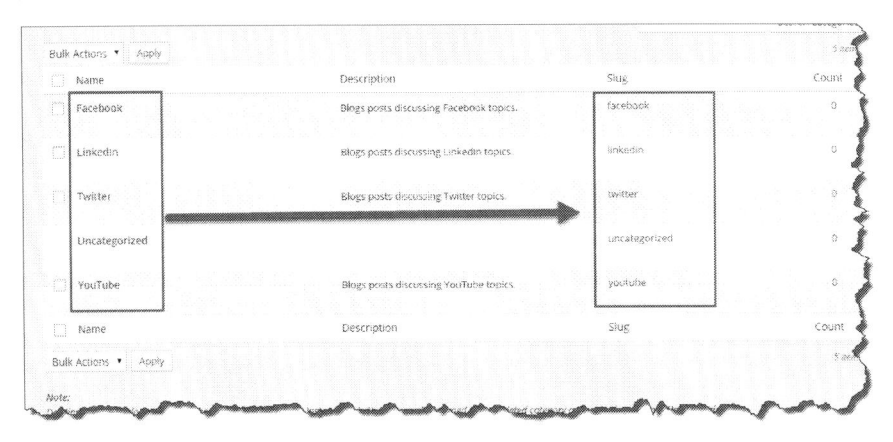

Note how **Name** uses upper case letters and **Slug** uses lower case letters.

Having created our **Categories**, we can now drop these into our **Posts** to signal our content type whenever we create a new post.

We can create new **Categories**, delete old ones (note that you don't lose the **Post** if you delete the Category) and change categories.

Tags Explained

Creating **Tags** is very similar to creating **Categories**.

In fact, creating most things in Wordpress will become a matter of routine quite fast once you get your blog underway.

When you break through that initial learning barrier, it's simply a case of repeating actions rather than having to continually learn new ones.

So what is the difference between **Categories** and **Tags**?

This is what Wordpress has to say:

Tags provide a useful way to group related posts together and to quickly tell readers what a post is about. Tags also make it easier for people to find your content. Tags are similar to but more specific than, categories. The use of tags is completely optional.

In very simple terms, tags are more descriptive, so by way of example, a category might be: Facebook

The tags associated with that category might be: personal profiles, business pages, Facebook ads, Facebook privacy, etc

Although you can create **Tags** beforehand, in the same way that you can create **Categories**, I tend to create my **Tags** alongside each post as I go along.

I find this a much better way to use them.

If you did want to manually create Tags, this is how you'd do it:

You would simply work through the Name - Slug – Description – Add New Tag process indicated in the image below.

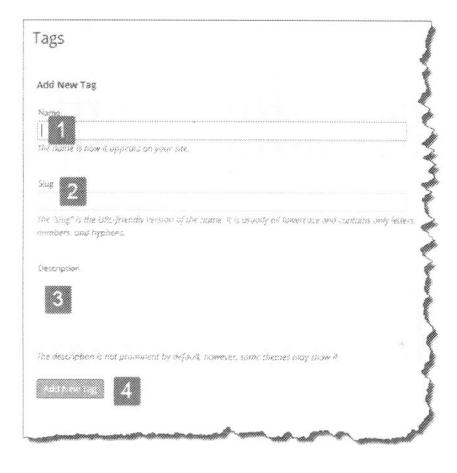

64

Once completed, your Tag would look like this:

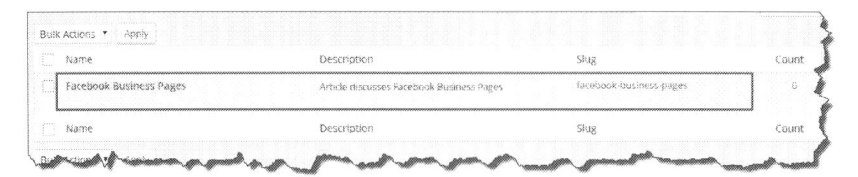

You can add Tags, delete them and edit them whenever you want to.

When we create our first post, though, you will see how easy it is to just add Tags as you go along and this is by far my preferred method.

Creating a New Post

Having set up our Categories, we can now create our first post.

There are two ways to do that:

If you use + **New** in the top menu, you'll be offered a selection of 5 options: Post/Media/Link/Page/User - in this case, select **Post**.

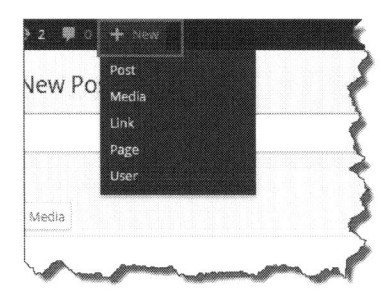

Alternatively, navigate to the left-hand menu, click **Posts** to open up the full posts menu, then select **Add New**:

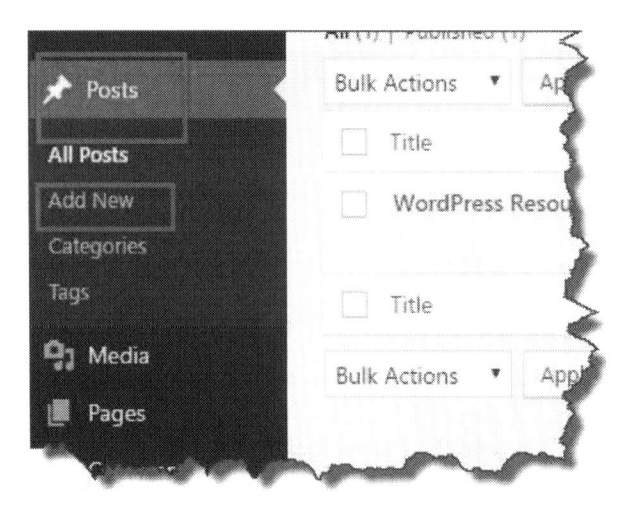

When you create your first Post, please ignore all the options on the right-hand side of the page for now. We'll work through those one at a time later on.

You need to focus on the **Add New Post** section first:

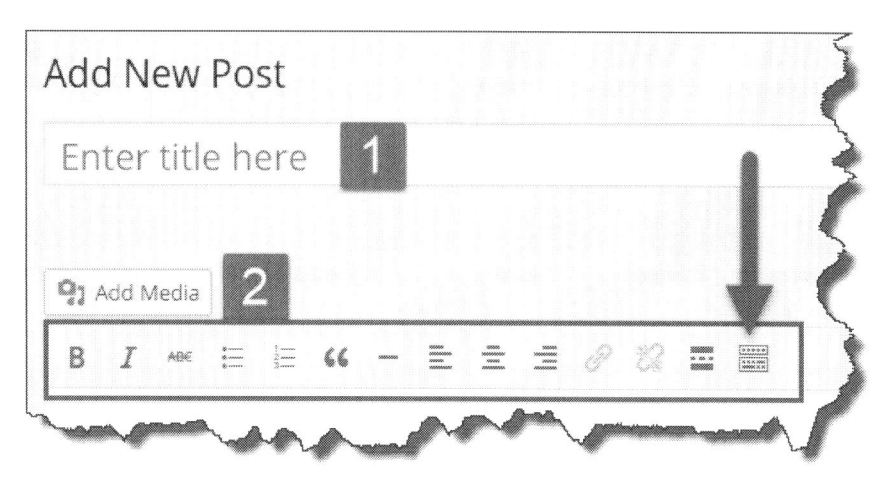

We're told to enter a title first and although this book is about using Wordpress rather than Search Engine Optimization and writing, here are two pointers:

- Make it attention grabbing (avoid being dull!)

- Try and include keywords (search engines love these!)

Ignore the **Add Media** button for now; we'll look at that in detail in a later chapter.

However, this is what you would use to add images to your new **Post**.

Below that **Add Media** button, we get **a Toolbar** which gives us a lot of useful functions.

In simple terms, this gives you the tools that you'd expect to see in, say Microsoft Word or a similar word-processing program.

If you click on the button on the far right-hand side (called 'Toolbar Toggle'), it will reveal another row of options to you:

Here's what those functions do for you, I'm working top row first, left to right, then bottom row left to right.

Top Row

Bold/Italic/Strikethrough/Bulleted List/Numbered List/Blockquote/Horizontal Line/Align Left/Align Centre/Align Right/Insert/Edit Link/Remove Link/Insert Read More Tag/Toolbar Toggle

Bottom Row

Text Format/Underline/Justify/Text Colour/Paste as Text/Clear Formatting/Special Character/Decrease Indent/Increase Indent/Undo/Redo/Keyboard Shortcuts

We can expand that Text Format drop-down menu a little more.

In that menu we are given the following options:

Paragraph/Address/Pre/Heading 1/ Heading 2/ Heading 3/ Heading 4/ Heading 5/ Heading 6

That looks like a very long list of permutations when it's presented like that.

However, when you get used to using Wordpress, it's just like the Word toolbar - very intuitive and simple to use.

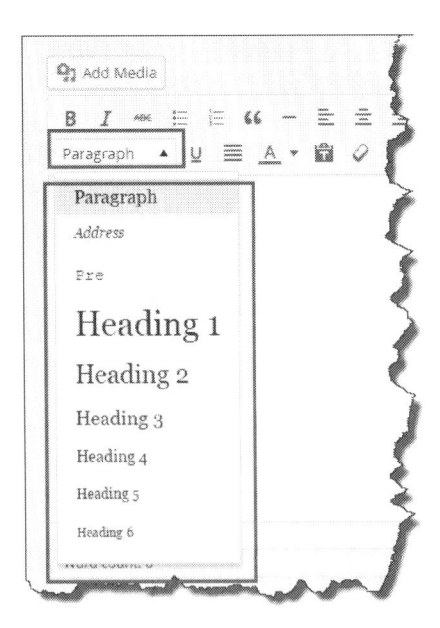

I would recommend that you have a play with the toolbar to see what everything does.

Just save the post as a draft (don't publish it if you don't want people to see it!), and you can then preview what it would look like.

You can't damage anything having a play like this, and only you can see your work so long as you don't click the **Publish** button.

Wordpress even gives you a handy **Word count** notification at the bottom of your Post:

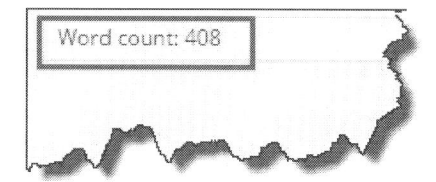

You may have noticed the **Visual/Text** tab on the right-hand side of your Post area:

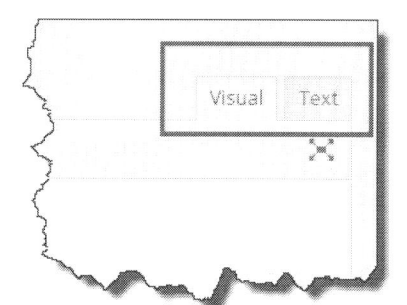

In Wordpress, you can work in WYSIWYG mode (What You See Is What You Get) or HTML mode.

You can flick between the modes whenever you want to:

Most of the time you won't even need to look at the Text view.

If you do, it probably means that you're adding a YouTube video or carrying out some other straightforward 'cut and paste' operation.

Just leave this area well alone if the thought of any sort of coding sends shivers up your spine!

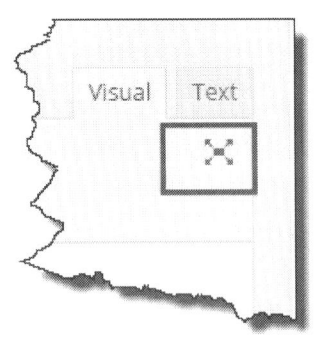

Underneath the Visual/Text tab is an unusual symbol.

This is for distraction free writing; it's just a simplified work area.

I have never used it, to be honest with you, but it's there if you ever need it.

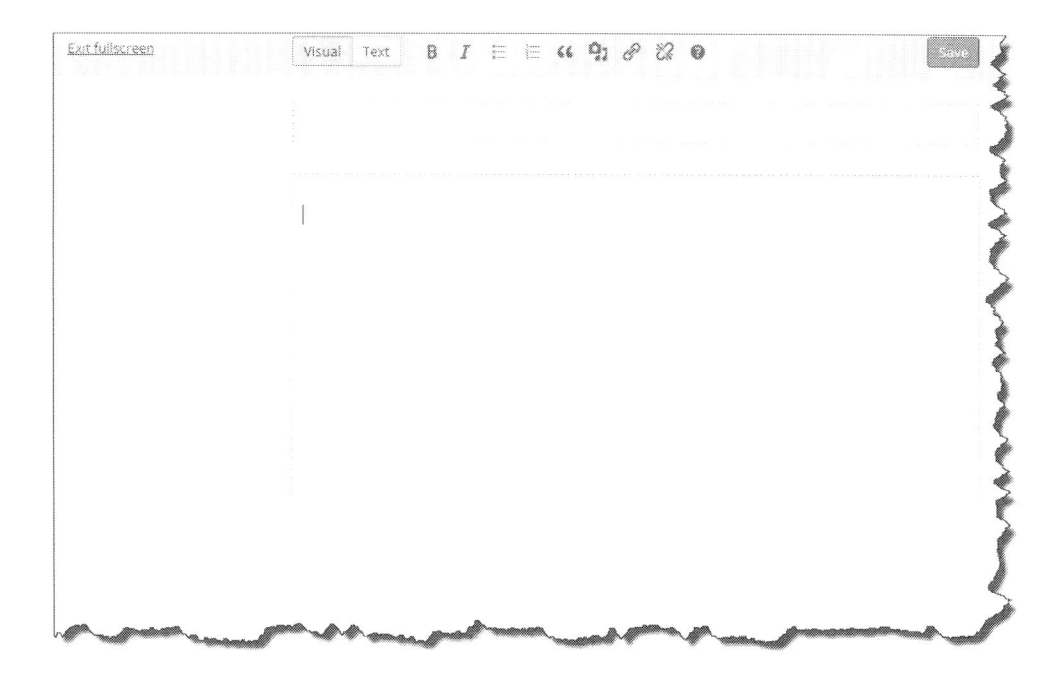

We now have a **Post** with some text and a title.

The next thing we need to do – prior to publication – is to allocate it to a **Category** and add some descriptive **Tags**.

To do that, move to the column on the right-hand side of the work area, and find **Categories**:

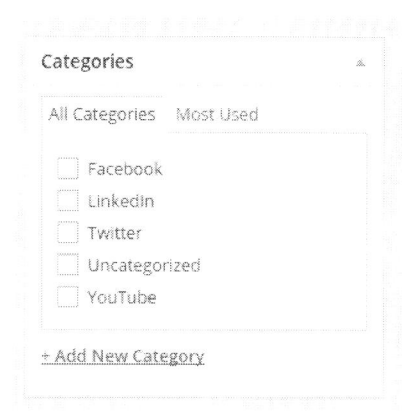

Simply click the most suitable category in your list of options, or click the + **Add New Category** link and add a new item to the list, without having to navigate away from the page that you are on.

Next, take a look at the **Tags** area.

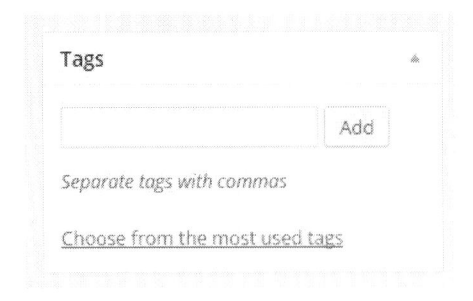

When I add **Tags**, I just skim my article and enter words or phrases which help to describe it best.

That's why I like to add my **Tags** as and when I need them, it works much better for me that way:

When you've been blogging for a while, that **Choose from the most used tags** link will be really useful.

Also, once you have lots of content on your site, you can use the built-in Tag Cloud widget which generates a fast-access, clickable area like this:

This is what that area looks like on my own blog, the most used tags being in the larger text:

With those jobs done, it's time to publish our **Post**.

Publish Options Explained

There are a number of options when it comes to publishing, but most of the time it will just be a straightforward operation.

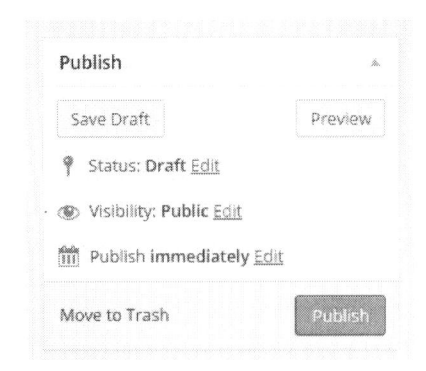

The most basic operation is **Save Draft** and **Preview**.

You'll do this while you're working on each post.

You can click that blue Publish button whenever you're ready for the world to read your completed post.

If you click on the **Edit** links, you open up some more possibilities.

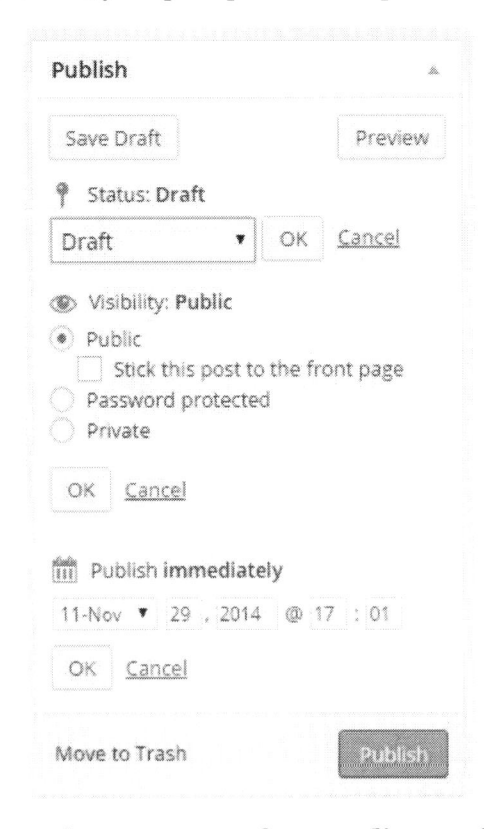

For instance, you can mark a post as a **Draft** or **Pending Review**.

You might use the second option if you have an editor who needs to check your work first:

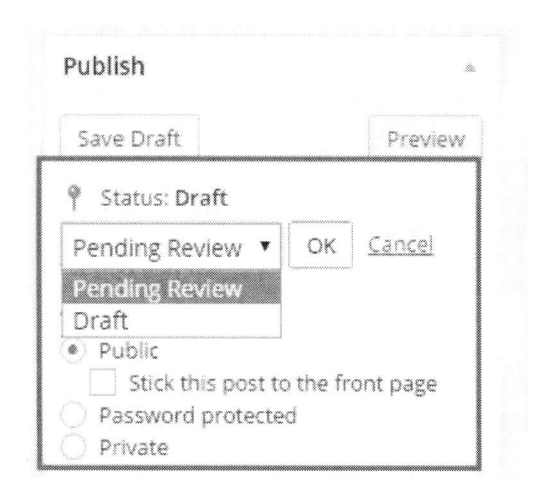

You can password protect posts, or make them private so that only you can see them.

By default, your posts should be **Public**.

The **Stick this post to the front page** option does just that, it defines a particular post which you want your readers to see.

Finally, you can publish your content on a specific date and time if you so wish, or you can just **Move to Trash**.

Most of the time, you'll just use **Draft** until the post is completed, then you'll **Publish**.

Format Options

You won't use **Format** options as a new Wordpress user, so just leave it at the default, i.e., **Standard** for the time being.

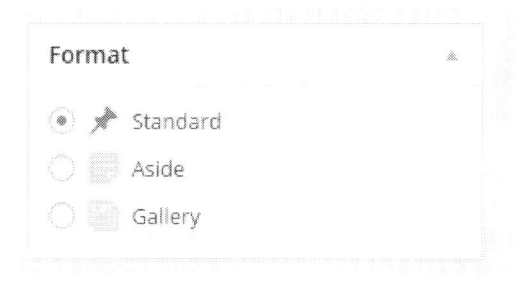

Featured Image

Some Wordpress themes use Featured Images; others don't.

Sometimes they need to be a specific size, other times they don't.

74

I would recommend leaving this alone – or adopting a spirit of free experimentation – but only after you've read the chapters on installing Wordpress themes and using Media in Wordpress.

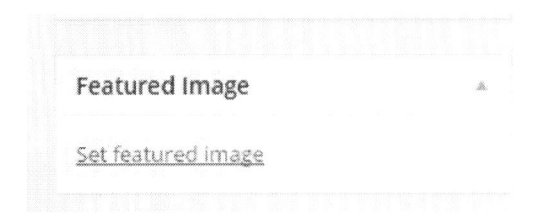

We have now created a Wordpress Post. When it comes to Pages the process is almost exactly the same, with just a few minor changes.

Creating a New Page

The menu process to create a brand new **Page** is almost the same as when we create a new **Post**.

Either start from the left-hand menu or click on **+New** at the top of the page.

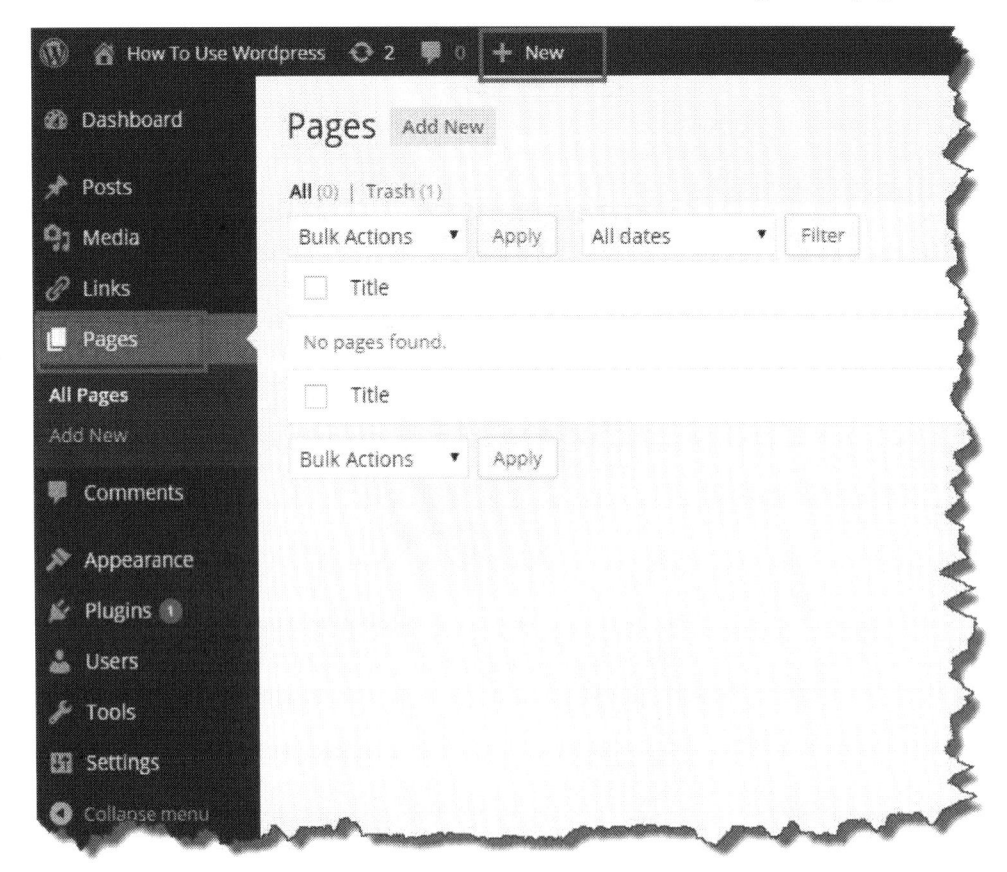

If you use **+ New** in the top menu, you'll be offered a selection of 5 options: Post/Media/Link/Page/User.

In this case, select **Page**.

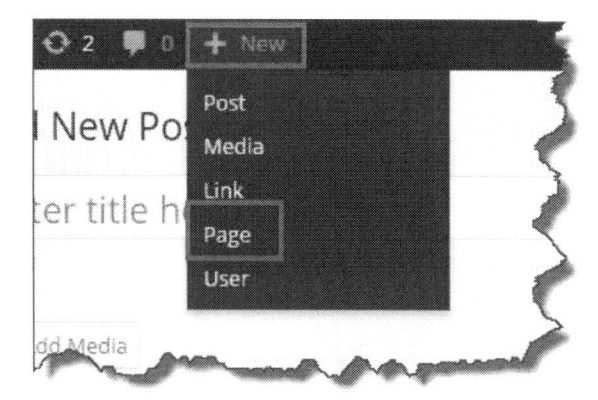

Your new **Page** works exactly the same as a **Post** in terms of actually creating content:

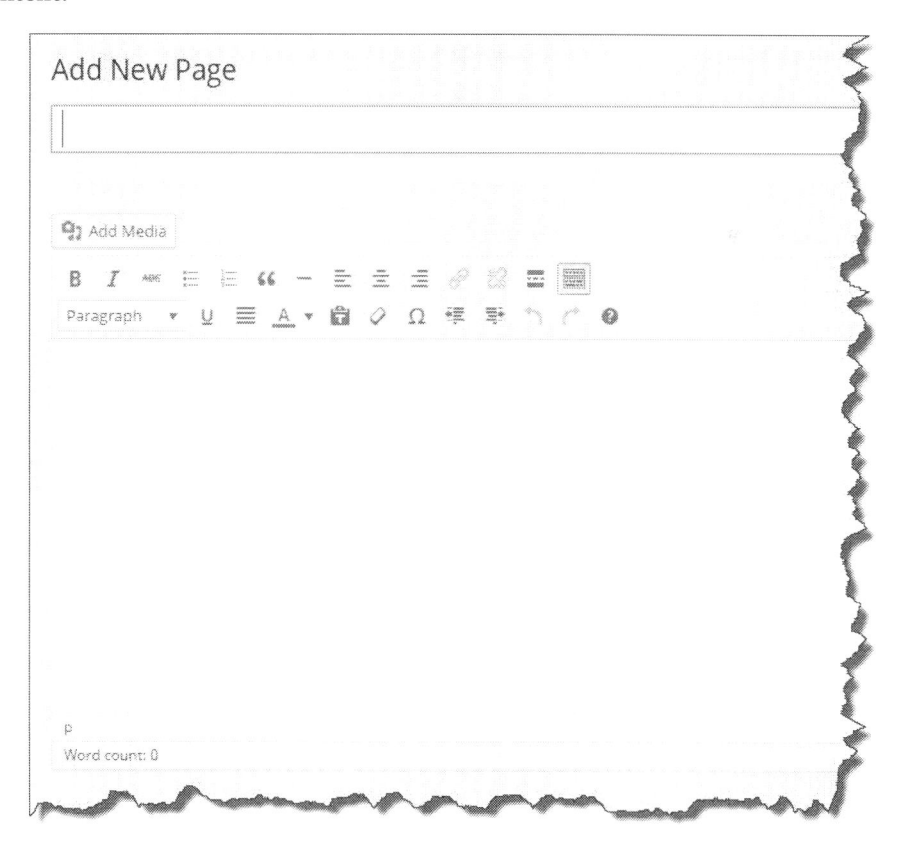

The **Toolbar** is the same, the word count is the same, and the Visual/Text tabs are the same.

It's only when you move over to the right-hand side that things change a little.

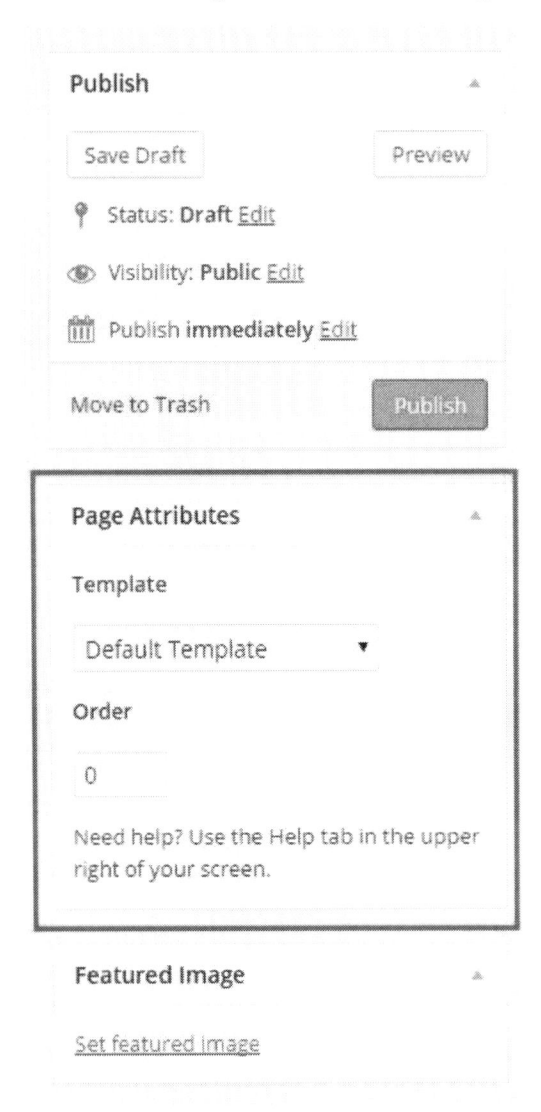

The **Publish** options are the same as for **Pages**.

The **Featured Image** option works in exactly the same way as it does for **Pages**.

Although **Page Attributes** does have some useful functionality, it's really not important at this very basic stage of operation:

I would suggest that with Pages, you just proceed as you did with Posts.

Create content, save it in **Draft** form, then **Publish** it when it's ready.

That's how I use Wordpress most of the time.

And that's it for Pages.

We don't use **Categories** and **Tags** because they're static pages, so don't let this confuse you.

With both pages and posts, you may be given the opportunity, depending on your Wordpress theme choice, to add a featured image:

Experiment with these. Sometimes they look great, at other times they can get in the way a bit – again, it all depends on which theme you decide to use.

Having created **Pages** and **Posts**, there's one final decision to make before we move onto **Media**.

That relates to what we're now going to show our blog visitors on our front page.

To sort out that issue, we have to return to the **Settings.**

The Front Page of Your Blog

Using the default theme that you are given with Wordpress (at the time of writing) you don't get a lot of options about what content is displayed.

To see the options available, in the left-hand menu, click on **Settings** then **Reading**:

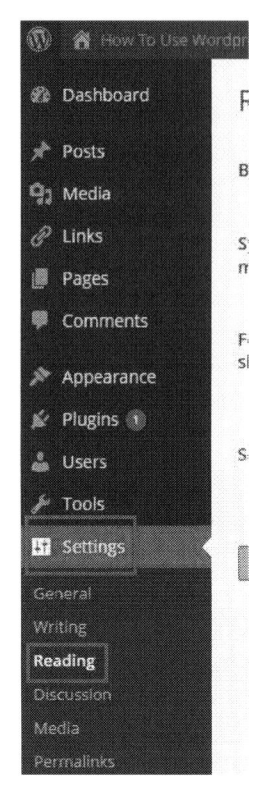

Most times, you don't really get any display options, just a choice of how many blog posts you can access via your blog's front page, with the default as 10.

You can also decide if you want to display the full post or just a summary:

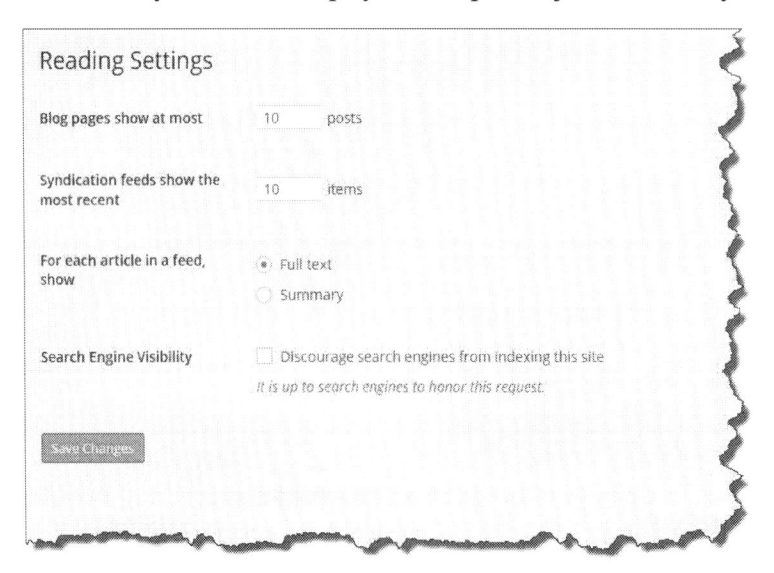

With more advanced theme options, you get a little more flexibility.

My own blog gives me the option to display Pages or Posts on my front page, and I can even select specific pages and posts:

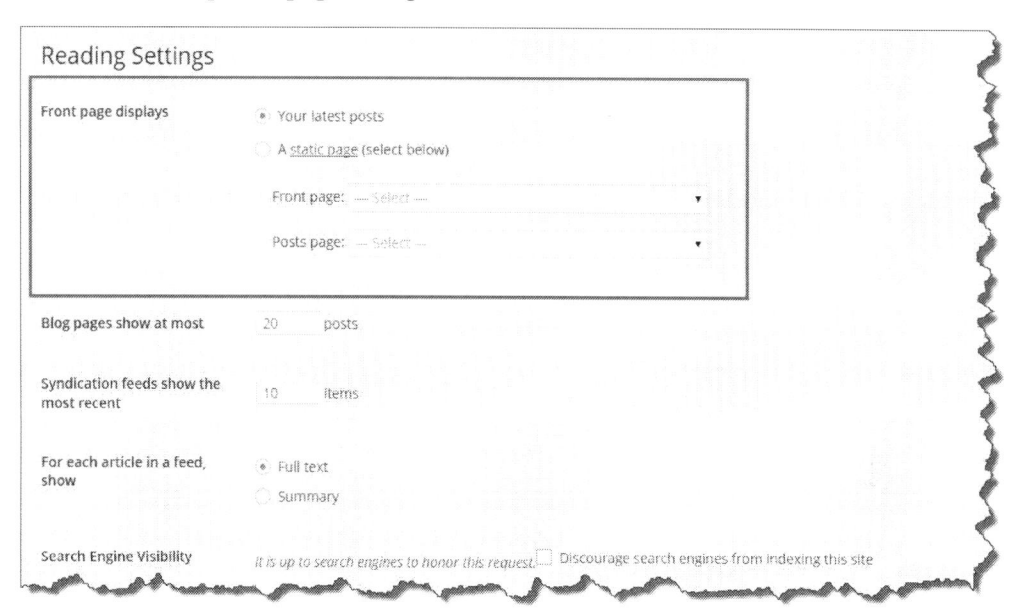

Reading Settings

Front page displays	● Your latest posts
	○ A static page (select below)
	Front page: — Select —
	Posts page: — Select —

Blog pages show at most: 20 posts

Syndication feeds show the most recent: 10 items

For each article in a feed, show: ● Full text ○ Summary

Search Engine Visibility: It is up to search engines to honor this request. ☐ Discourage search engines from indexing this site

The key point to make here is that you need to be flexible. It depends on your choice of theme for your blog, but just be aware that you do need to check out this area to see if you can do anything a bit more advanced.

The options may vary from what you see here, but have a mindset of experimentation beforehand. It's very difficult to do permanent damage on Wordpress.

You can now create Posts and Pages on your new Wordpress blog.

I hope that already you're beginning to see how easy this is.

Chapter 7: Using Media Files

At the time of writing, self-installed Wordpress sites support the following file types:

Images

.jpg

.jpeg

.png

.gif

Documents

.pdf (Portable Document Format; Adobe Acrobat)

.doc, .docx (Microsoft Word Document)

.ppt, .pptx, .pps, .ppsx (Microsoft PowerPoint Presentation)

.odt (OpenDocument Text Document)

.xls, .xlsx (Microsoft Excel Document)

.zip

Audio

.mp3

.m4a

.ogg

.wav

Video

.mp4, .m4v (MPEG-4)

.mov (QuickTime)

.wmv (Windows Media Video)

.avi

.mpg

.ogv (Ogg)

.3gp (3GPP)

.3g2 (3GPP2)

I think that's a pretty impressive range of options.

However, you are limited by the size of the file that your web hosting service will allow you to upload.

That is often 4MB by default, which doesn't give you a lot of scope for audio and video files in most cases.

Depending on your hosting package, you can get the file upload size increased; mine is currently at 64MB.

In addition, I would always put audio onto a 3rd party service like https://soundcloud.com/ and video into a service like https://www.youtube.com/.

For all sorts of cost-based, technical and delivery reasons, that's a far better way to deal with very big file types.

With that said, we'll take a look now at the two file formats that you can use easily with Wordpress.

The one that I can guarantee that you'll use in most cases is images.

Getting Started With Wordpress Media

There are two ways to use Wordpress **Media**.

You can either navigate directly to that area and add your files one-by-one or, what is more common when you have used Wordpress for some time, is to just add your files directly into **Posts** and **Pages**.

When you manually add your files, you navigate to the Media section in exactly the same way that we reached Posts and Pages earlier.

We do this via the left-hand menu or the + **New** link at the top of the Wordpress work area:

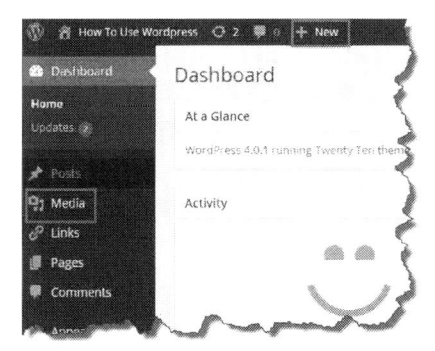

From the + **New** link you can access Media in the short drop-down menu:

Once inside the Media area, the first time you go there will be nothing there, just a message announcing **No media attachments found**.

To get things underway, click on the **Add New** link:

Uploading Media Files

Once you have clicked on that **Add New** link, you will see how Wordpress facilitates file uploads.

You'll get very used to this format; it's exactly the same when you upload files manually, as we are doing now, and when you upload them from within **Posts** and **Pages**.

We have two options with the uploader (see image below)

1 – Drag and drop our files directly onto the uploader

2 – Click on the **Select Files** buttons and browse to the files

Method 1 may sound like the coolest technique to use but, in my day-to-day work, I tend to use Method 2 mostly.

Note (3 in the image on the next page) that my maximum file upload size is 64 MB. I had that increased by my web host, it's usually much less than that.

If you find that you're trying to upload files that won't be accepted by Wordpress due to their size, it's time to drop your web host a support desk ticket to ask for an increase.

I think that the most I use routinely is no more than 20 MB, if you want an indication of a decent increase to request.

The reason that I don't use the 'drop files' method is that it requires you to minimize windows, and that's not the way I work most of the time.

I would use it to bulk upload images, but most of the time I add them one-by-one.

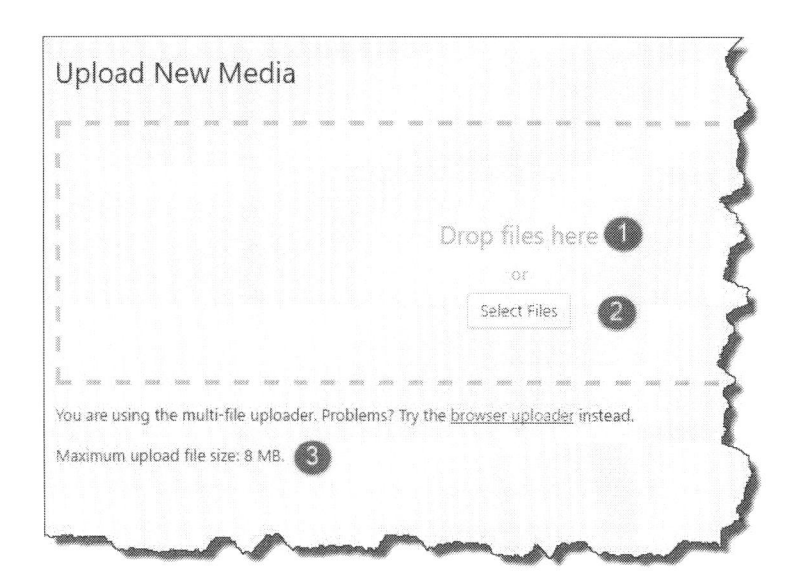

The other reason for adding them one-by-one is that labelling images correctly is a great way of improving site SEO (Search Engine Optimization).

Never label your images image001.jpg, picture1.gif or anything undescriptive like those two examples.

Instead, label them descriptively with keywords, as this helps the search engines to know what your content is all about.

Better labels would be daffodil-flower.jpg or blue-winter-coat.gif.

You'd be surprised how much 'SEO power' correctly labelled images can add.

This is what you would do to drag and drop your images; you'd click on the images that you wanted to upload, then drag them across to the **Drop files anywhere to upload** area:

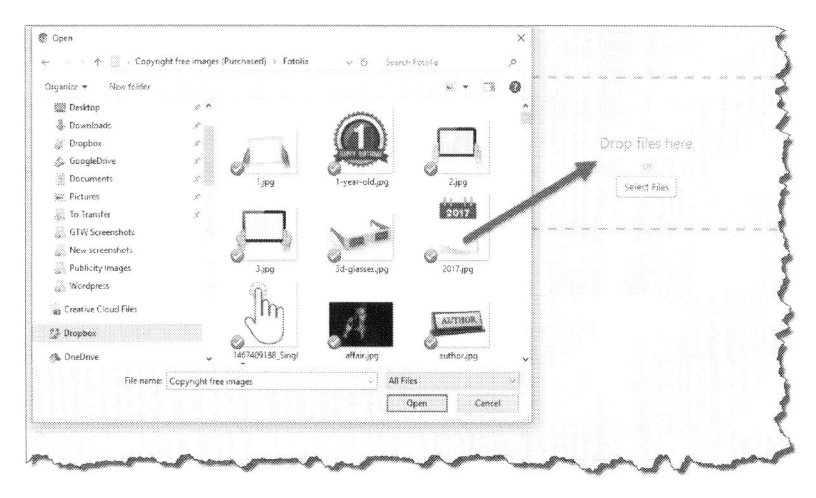

As the images upload, you'll see progress bars showing you how long you have to go until the process is completed:

Once the upload is complete, Wordpress will generate a thumbnail of the images:

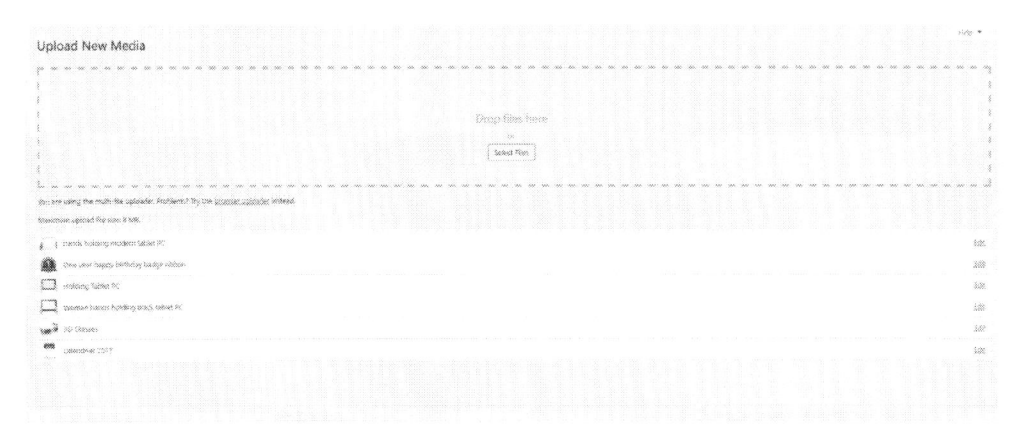

Now that was all very quick, of course, but to do things properly you still have to click on each image individually to make sure that you have completed all of the associated data correctly.

That's why I do them one at a time; it just works better for me.

Labelling Images

The next step is to label the images.

You may be tempted to be a bit lazy at this point - believe me, I have been too at times - but the simple truth is, the better you label your images, the more it will help your blog to perform well in the search engines.

This is a job that is tempting to skip, but which will pay dividends in the long term.

When I was running a BBC website in 2010, over 50% of the site's search results were coming from correctly labelled images.

As a locally based site, we'd uploaded hundreds of images showing local communities.

Because we'd described those images correctly, it brought in many, many users because they could be so easily located in the search engines.

If we'd just labelled them all image001.jpg, image002.jpg, etc. nobody would ever have been able to find them properly via a search engine query.

To start to label your images, just click on one of those thumbnails:

You'll notice that you get a lot of data before you even begin (indicated by 1 in the above image), such as file name, file type, upload date, file size and image dimensions.

That data was all fixed at the point of upload.

There is now some essential work to be done in the section below that (marked by 2-7 in the image above).

URL – this is the direct link to your image. You just uploaded it to your server, so you can now share it as a web link if you wish to (2).

Title – Sometimes, if you use stock images from sites like https://en.fotolia.com/ (a recommended site by the way) it will have a ready-made title (3).

If not, create one and if you don't like the one that you've been given, change it.

The title is primarily there to help you identify your images.

Caption – This is a very short description of your image which will be displayed publicly (4).

Alt Text – This is really important, it is an accessibility issue on your blog (5).

When people use screen reader software, maybe because they have a visual impairment, the alt tag describes what the image is all about.

So make it descriptive, as if you were describing to somebody on the telephone what you're looking at.

So your alt text might be 'Picture of a family house in Lisbon' or 'A young man cycling quickly in a race.'

We don't need a 'War and Peace' description. The simple rule for writing alt tags is 'Say what you see.'

Description – This will create a bordered text area for your image, so you may or may not wish to use it, depending on your content (6, in the image on the previous page).

The rule of thumb with images is that the more description that you give, the better things will be for SEO.

Don't go overboard, but one thing is for certain if you never move beyond image001.jpg and image002.jpg, the SEO on your site is likely to be poor.

This is how your image description might look once completed:

URL	http://web-work-at-home.com/demo/wp-content/uploads/.
Title	Coming soon signboard
Caption	Coming soon signboard
Alt Text	A green ignboard with the words 'Coming Soon'
Description	A signboard with the words 'Coming Soon'
Uploaded By	PaulTeague

Please note that I have been descriptive but brief. My main identifying keyword here is 'signboard' and I have been consistent in my use of that word.

Having labelled our image correctly, we can now move on to editing it, if required.

Just a note about this final menu (7 in the image two pages back), which you'll notice in the editing area.

There's not much of major interest here so I would encourage you to click the links (not **Delete Permanently** of course!) and get a feel for them, but you'll probably never use them again.

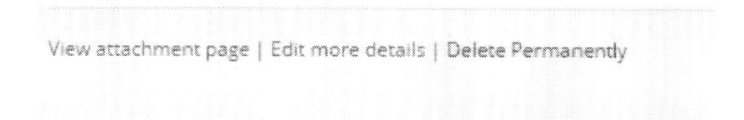

View attachment page | Edit more details | Delete Permanently

Editing Images

The next step is to edit the image itself.

If for whatever reason, you have navigated away from the image that you were editing, you can easily get back to it.

All of the images that you just uploaded are now available in the (previously empty) Media Library.

Just click on the image that you want to edit to pick up where you left off.

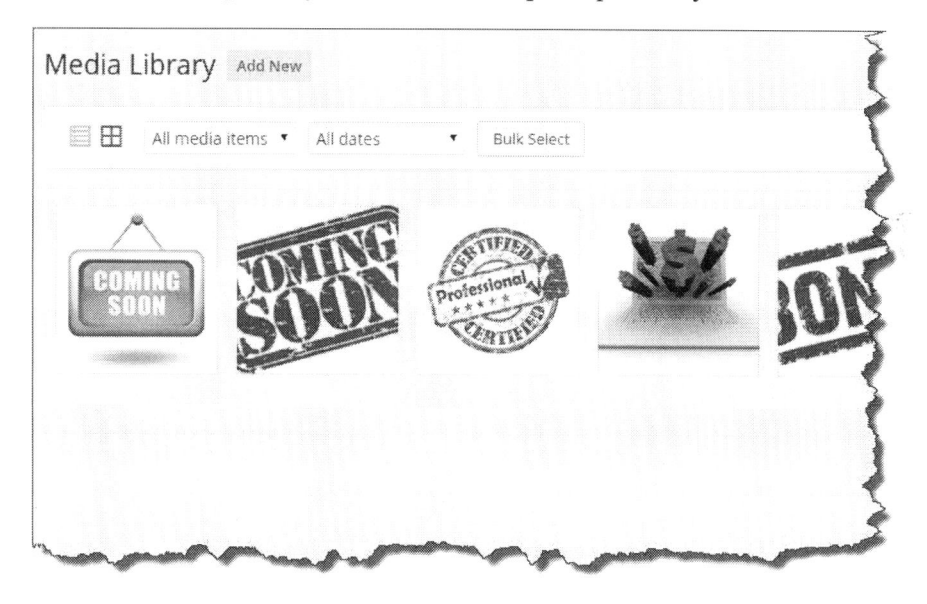

Having opened up the image, click on the **Edit Image** button below the image preview:

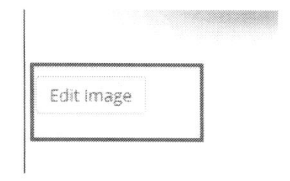

This is what the edit image button looks like in context when working with a picture:

This now opens up two new menus to you:

There's no fancy image editing is required when you use Wordpress, that's just one more advantage of using this excellent software.

You may crop the image (1), rotate it left or right (2), flip vertically or horizontally (3), undo and redo (4) and, of course, save (5) as illustrated in the full screenshot shown on the next page:

Media File Sizes

The menu on the right-hand side of the work area gives you yet more options related to re-sizing and re-scaling the image.

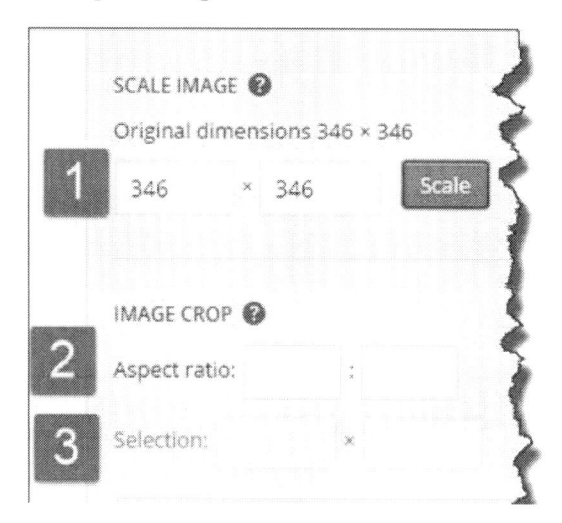

Scale Image

Wordpress says: *You can proportionally scale the original image. For best results, scaling should be done before you crop, flip, or rotate. Images can only be scaled down, not up.*

90

Image Crop

<u>Wordpress says</u>: *To crop the image, click on it and drag to make your selection.*

Crop Aspect Ratio

The aspect ratio is the relationship between the width and height. You can preserve the aspect ratio by holding down the shift key while resizing your selection. Use the input box to specify the aspect ratio, e.g. 1:1 (square), 4:3, 16:9, etc.

Crop Selection

Once you have made your selection, you can adjust it by entering the size in pixels. The minimum selection size is the thumbnail size as set in the Media settings.

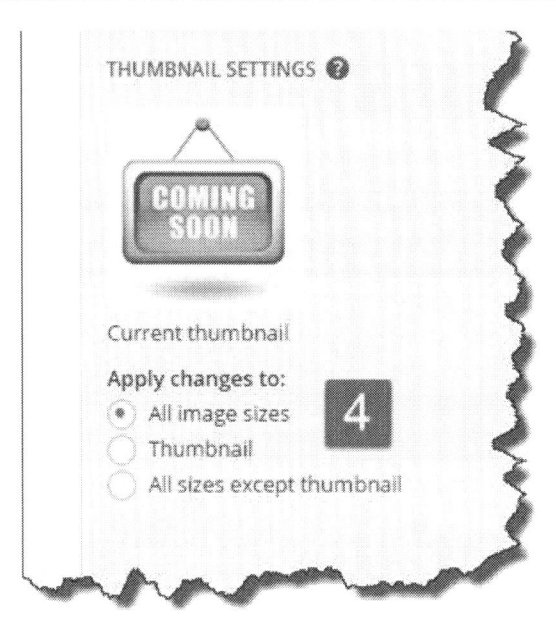

Thumbnail settings

<u>Wordpress says</u>: *You can edit the image while preserving the thumbnail. For example, you may wish to have a square thumbnail that displays just a section of the image.*

Always remember to **Save** your changes as you go along.

Inserting Media Files Into Pages and Posts

Having talked you through this process, I barely ever manipulate my images using that particular technique.

It's much more usual to add and edit your images directly within a **Page** or **Post**.

91

For this demonstration, I will demonstrate via **Posts** as that is how you will be creating content most of the time.

However, it's exactly the same process when you add images to **Pages**, nothing changes.

Start by creating a **Page** in the normal way:

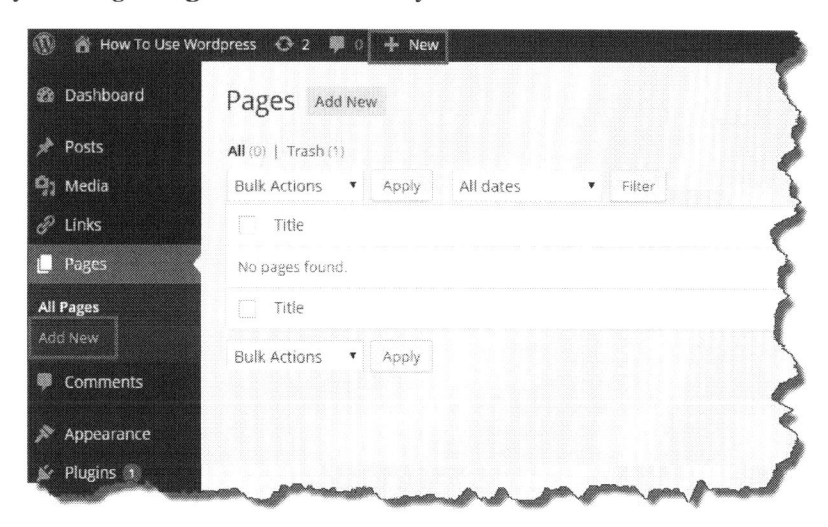

For this example, I am going to demonstrate how to upload and insert an image into some text, so that you can also see how to wrap an image correctly.

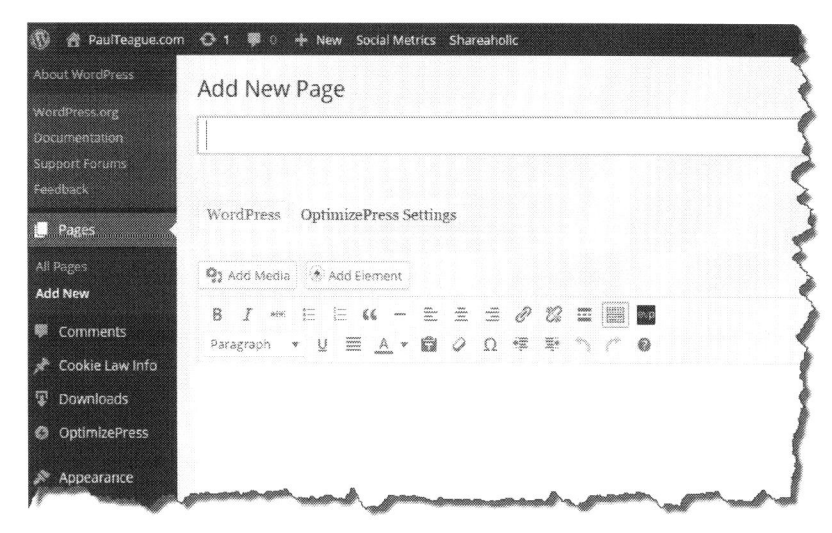

To get started, place your cursor where you want the image to be placed, then click on **Add Media**.

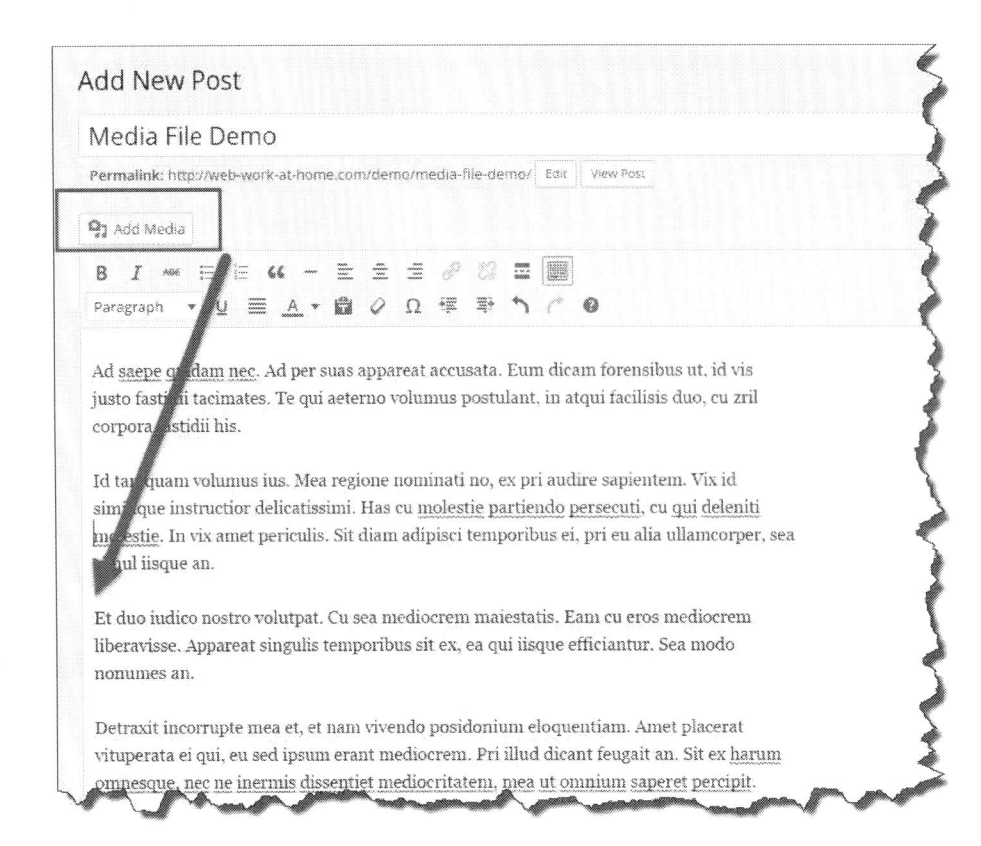

The next page should look familiar to you already, or, at least, the **Drop files anywhere to upload/Select files** will from when we manually uploaded images earlier:

You may have some additional options in the left-hand navigation, such as **Create Gallery** or **Set Featured Image**.

I'm not going to explore those options in this book, which is geared to giving you only those skills which you need to make a fast start with Wordpress.

You can even **Insert from URL** if you want to, but beware infringing copyright if you use this technique.

The images that you use for this technique ought to be hosted on your own server and be your own copyright. If not, they're best avoided.

The process for uploading is (1) Select Files (2) Click on your chosen image (3) Click Open or whichever button completes the upload process on your PC.

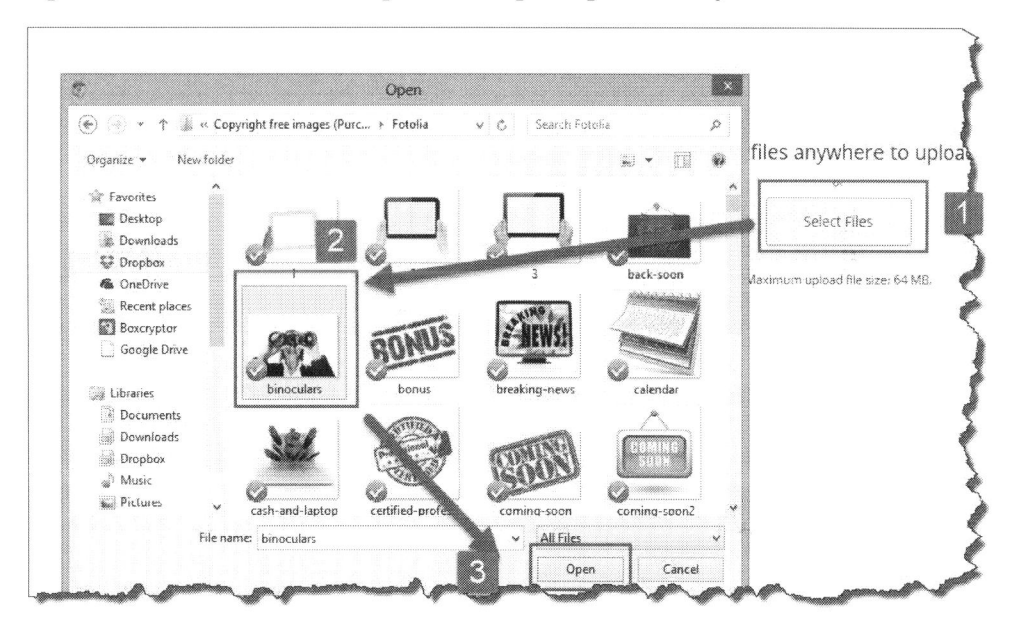

We now have to go through the process of inserting a title/caption/alt text and description.

The next option using this image insertion technique is **Attachment Display Settings**.

Wordpress does something that is very annoying at this stage; it automatically inserts a link to the media file.

You don't actually want that. You need to remove the link and, when you've been using Wordpress for a while, this gets a bit wearing.

There is a way to stop this happening, using a free **Plugin,** so I will save this operation for that chapter.

For now, we'll live with it. It is easily corrected at least, and it's a good opportunity to make you aware of this issue and how to put it right.

94

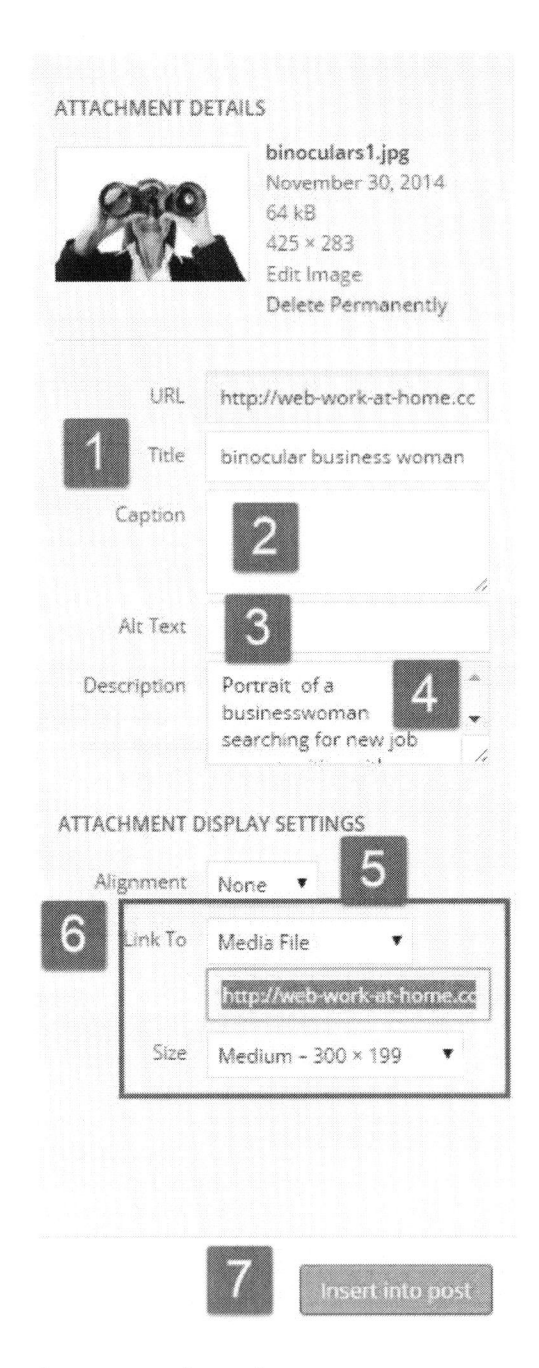

In the **Link To** drop-down menu, just select **None**.

This means that when a blog visitor clicks on the image, it won't take them away from the page that they're on.

It's an unnecessary step, and I'm not really sure why Wordpress still forces it.

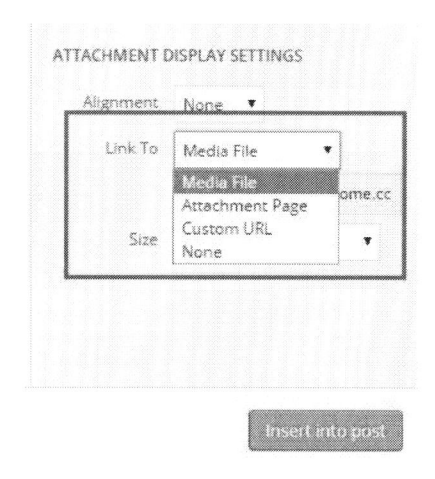

Having removed that link, we can now attend to the **Size** drop-down menu.

We have three choices here:

A thumbnail

A medium size (reduced) image

A full size (original) image

Select which one suits you best and be mindful that we can adjust that size in the next step, when we view the image in the context of having our text placed around it.

I often find that this is the best stage at which to do the tweaking, so I keep the image at a reasonable size and adjust it on the page.

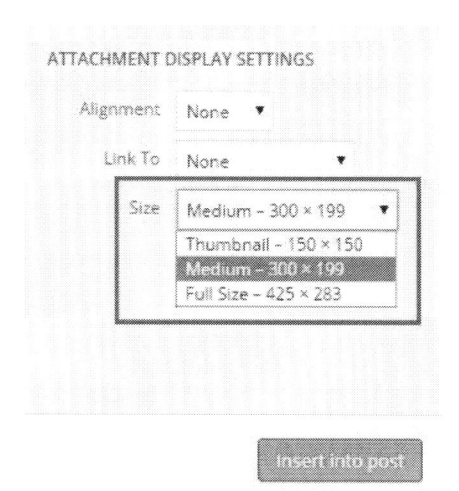

We still need to **Insert into post** of course, and that's done by clicking on the relevant button:

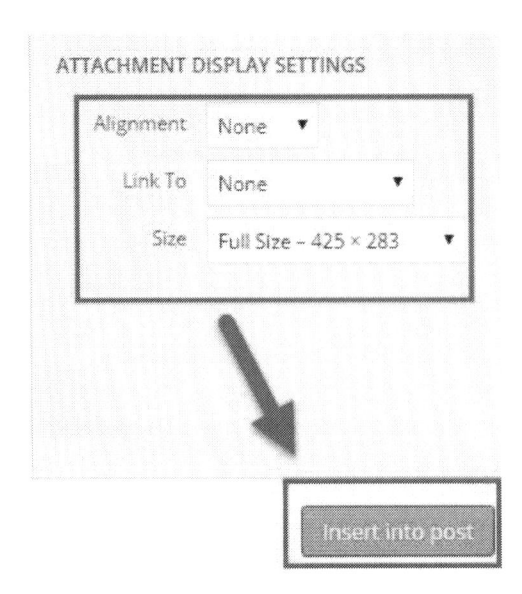

You will now be returned to your original **Post,** where you can now see exactly how that image looks on the page.

The text will not be wrapped by default; we'll need to manually force that if indeed it's what you want.

Sometimes I keep larger images centred because they just look better on the page like that.

You'll notice that in your admin view (your blog visitors won't see them in the published version) you get a pencil icon and a cross icon on the top left-hand side of the image.

To align or further adjust the image, just click on the pencil icon. To remove the image from the post, simply click on the cross icon.

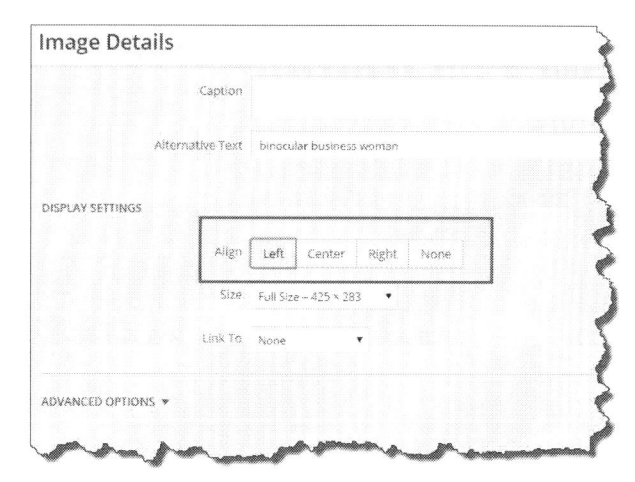

We can further adjust the image now, and it's particularly important to get the alignment correct.

I usually alternate left and right alignment down a blog post, with large images, centred.

It makes a blog post look pleasing to the eye in that it is balanced and even.

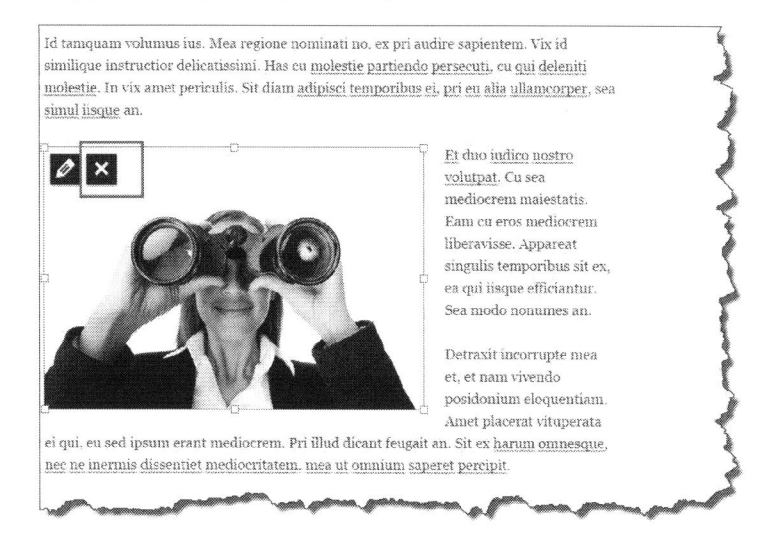

Once you have aligned your image, the text will wrap around it correctly so that it looks much better on the page.

A Final Word on Images

That's really all there is to it when adding images to your blog's **Posts** or **Pages**.

It really is very straightforward and, of course, as you upload more and more images, you begin to build a large image library in your Media area, and you can use those in your content any time you please.

One final word about images and that relates to copyright.

You are not allowed to just help yourself to other peoples' images, that is a breach of their copyright.

The safest way to approach this matter is just to use images that you have taken yourself, on your own camera.

However, that becomes very restrictive.

So, to make sure that you get this right, please use a stock photo service such as https://en.fotolia.com/ the one that I use mostly, as the images are cheap and high quality.

There are many free services available, but the images are of a lower quality on the whole and I would recommend that you give your blog a quality 'look and feel' right from the outset.

Adding Other Media Files

My recommendation to you is going to be that you use YouTube and SoundCloud for audio and video, but I will save more advanced matters like that for a second book, where we can get a little more ambitious with our blog.

I will, however, show you how to upload files such as .pdfs and .docs as this is very similar to the process with images, with just a few small alterations.

First of all, repeat the process to create a new blog **Post** or **Page.**

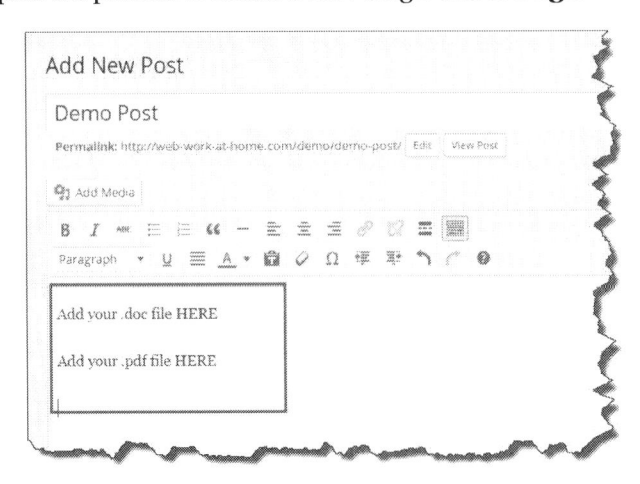

In my example, I am assuming that we want to add two common file types to a page so that the files can be downloaded by blog readers.

We click on **Add Media**, exactly the same as with images, to access the uploader tool.

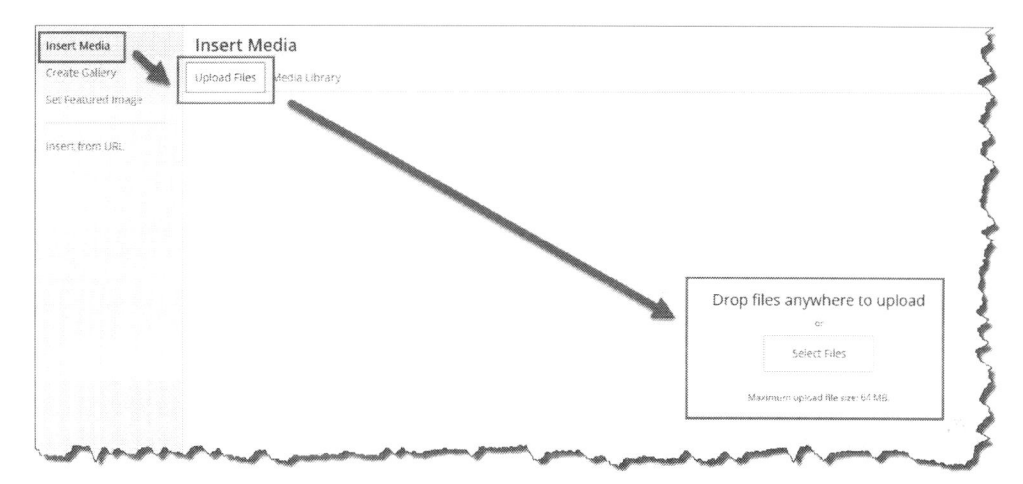

Remember, your files may be larger than the **Maximum upload file size** that your web host allows, so you may be restricted from uploading larger files without first requesting an increase in your capped limit.

My 64 MB allowance is not typical; your upload allocation will likely be much lower by default, so please be aware of this limitation.

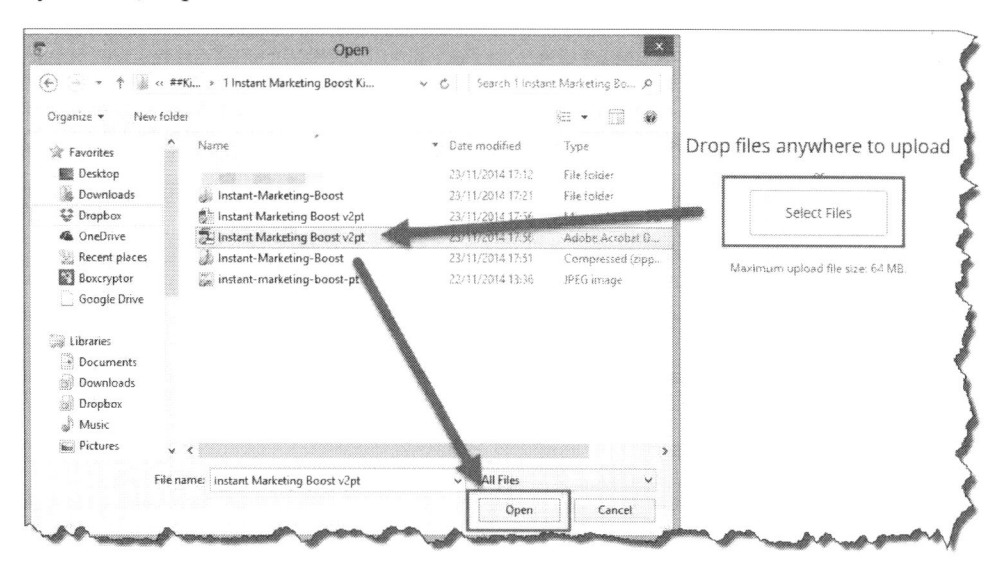

Click the **Select Files** button, navigate to your document, then click the **Open** button or whatever the equivalent is on your own PC or laptop.

Your file, whatever file type it is, is simply added to your **Media Library** where you can now access it at any time.

Just click the **Insert into file** button, and a link is placed in your blog post:

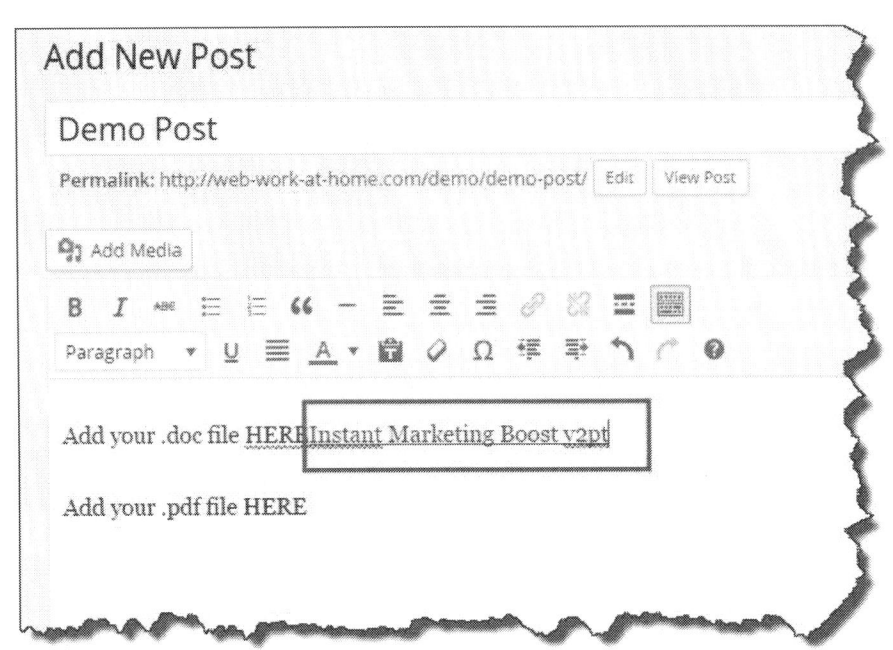

It works exactly the same with a .doc file and any other *permitted* file type that you upload:

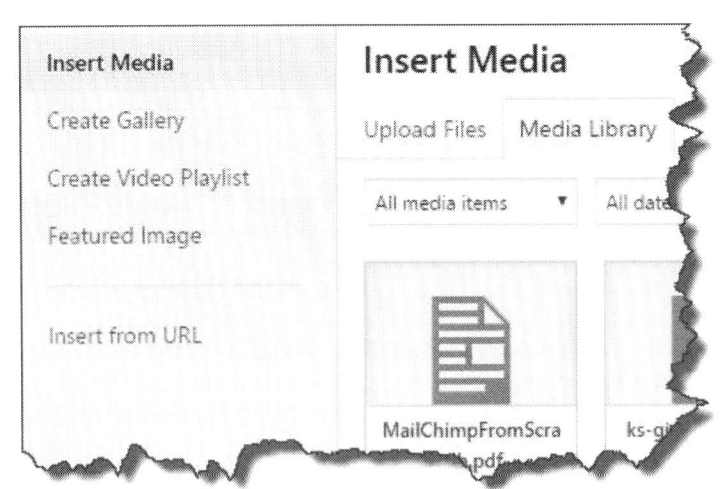

This really is a tech-free and very intuitive process. Once you've done it a few times, you'll be able to do this really fast.

I'll just flag up at this stage that these files are browsable by those who know where to look, and they are also indexed by search engines, so it is best not to upload anything confidential or private.

You need to delve a little deeper into file protection and membership protected areas to solve those problems, but I'll save that for a more advanced Wordpress guide.

At the moment, that page does not look very nice; we need to make an adjustment.

There are two ways that you can do this.

The link takes on the title of the document, so the really simple way is to rename the document *before* you upload it from your PC or laptop.

The alternative - and quick way - to do it is to place the words that you want inside the existing text.

We do this so that we don't mess up or break the link to the file.

We then delete the words that we don't want, leaving everything looking neat, tidy and easy for our readers to use.

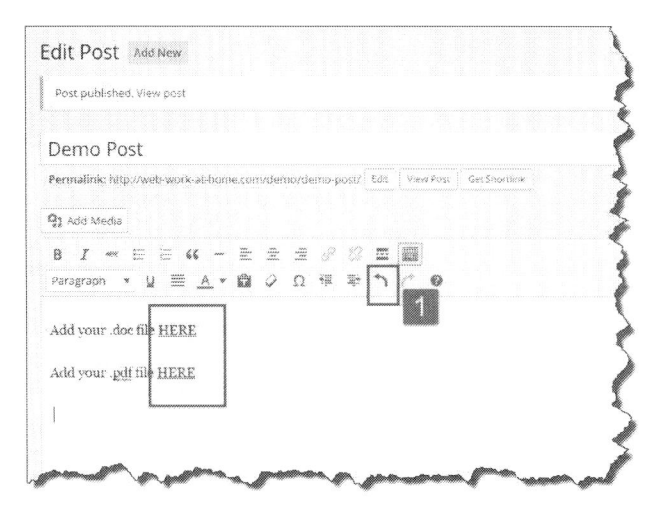

If you mess this up and break the linked text, just click on the **Undo** arrow in the **Toolbar** (marked 1 in the image above).

There is just one final Ninja tip to show you when it comes to documents.

When you preview that page, or publish it and view it as your blog readers see it, you will notice that when you click on those links it takes you away from the blog itself.

In web terms, that is not a good thing; we want to keep our readers on our blog as long as possible.

So I always set external links (i.e., sites that take the reader away from my own blog) to **open in a new window**.

To do that, click on the web link that you want to change. You'll observe in the Toolbar that the link icons change colour slightly:

Click on the left-hand link icon, and a window will pop up on your screen:

Simply check the box next to **Open link in a new window/tab**, then click the **Update** button and the job is done.

Repeat this action for each link that you want to open in a new window.

Remember to save the **Post** or **Page** once you have changed all of the links to ensure that the changes you just made are stored.

You can now add images and document files to your **Posts** and **Pages** in Wordpress.

Chapter 8: Changing the Appearance of Your Blog

One of the best things about Wordpress is your ability as a user to completely change the appearance of your site in, literally, just a few minutes.

When I started blogging, I used a free theme for about a year if I remember correctly.

I then purchased a theme which was widely used in my industry, and it served me well for the next few years.

Then I became aware of the importance of my blog displaying correctly on smartphones and other mobile devices, so I installed another purchased theme called Optimizepress at https://www.optimizepress.com/.

In my opinion, Optimizepress is the best mobile responsive theme for online marketers to use, but you need to give it a wide berth as a completely new user to Wordpress. It's quite complex and definitely not for you until you have some experience with the platform.

In fact, it has taken me some time to master version 2 of Optimizepress, and I'm still figuring out the advanced membership options.

However, the more I use it, the more I love it.

Right now, we're going to look at the hundreds of free (and straightforward!) themes that have been created for Wordpress, and I'll show you the best places to go if you want to pay for a better-looking theme.

What is a Theme?

This is what Wordpress has to say about themes:

A WordPress Theme is a collection of files that work together to produce a graphical interface with an underlying unifying design for a weblog. These files are called template files. A Theme modifies the way the site is displayed, without modifying the underlying software.

Put simply; a theme determines how your blog looks and the things that you can do behind the scenes.

The great thing about Wordpress – yet another one – is that you can change themes every day of the week if you want to. You lose none of your content when you do so.

It will *look* different of course – that's why you changed your theme – but you lose no content when you change a theme. It's just the appearance and layout of your blog which changes.

So that means whenever you want to make a change, you can, and there are hundreds of themes available for free, in all shapes and sizes.

We navigate to themes via the left-hand main menu, then select **Appearance** and **Themes**.

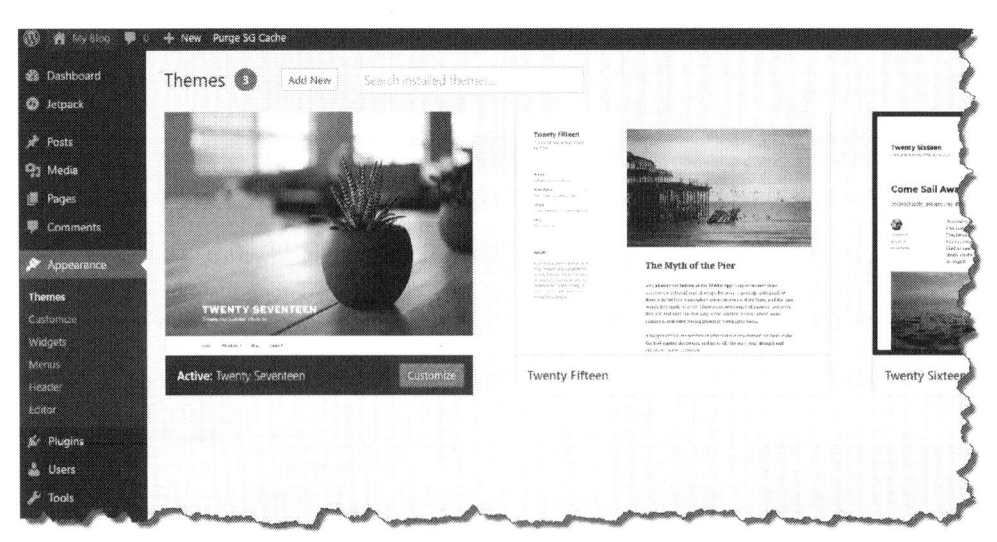

When you install Wordpress for the first time, you will be given some default themes (1 in the image above).

At the time of writing, my installation gives me:

- Twenty Seventeen Theme

- Twenty Sixteen Theme

- Twenty Fifteen Theme

The Twenty Seventeen Theme was installed by default.

You can also **Add New Theme** (see image below) at the click of a button; it is extremely easy to do.

You can also delete themes and – not for this book – edit and adapt the code to each theme.

Why Pay for Themes?

I began using a free theme and swiftly moved on to paid themes, where I have stayed ever since.

In fact, I use version 2 of Optimizepress on several blog installations at the time of writing.

I also use and love Thrive Themes at https://thrivethemes.com/.

The reality of using free themes is that they are usually not updated as often as they should be, so you may find that they 'break' or create technical issues whenever Wordpress rolls out one of its regular updates.

It really is a case of 'you get what you pay for' I'm afraid, but I still maintain that you're best off learning Wordpress via free themes.

You'll know when it's time to move on because you'll want your theme to do more and more as you become increasingly more familiar with the software.

Where to Find Free Themes

There are two main techniques for finding free Wordpress themes.

Firstly, you can just click on that large, circular + sign to **Add New Theme**:

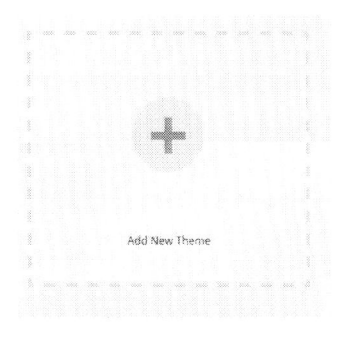

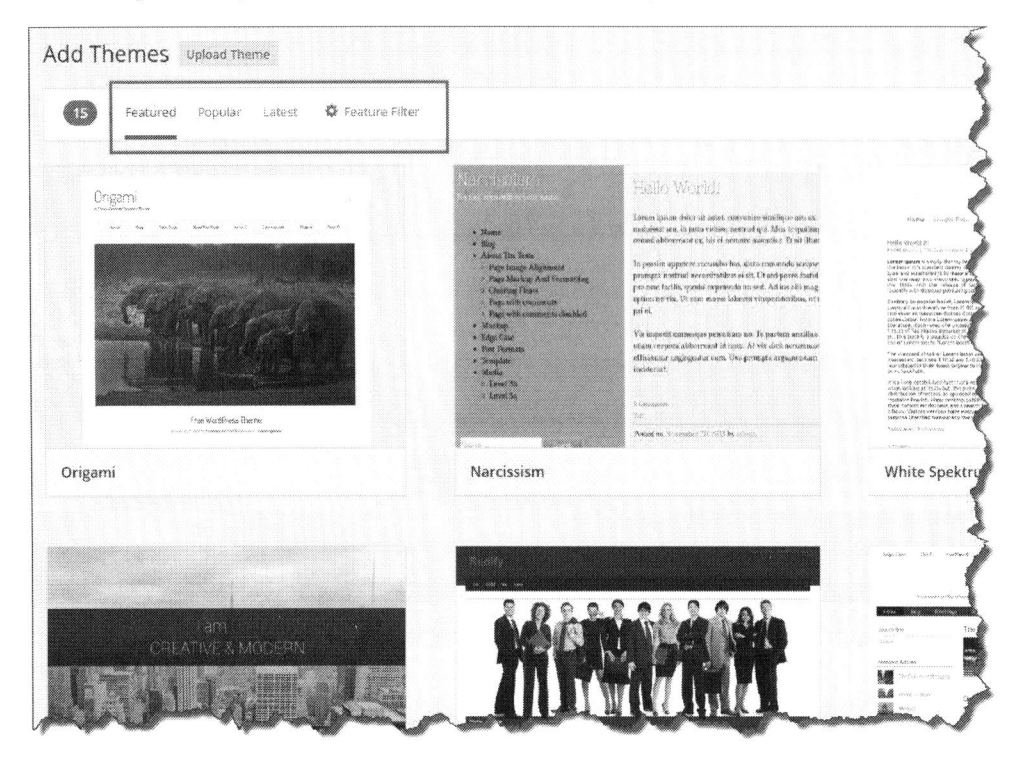

That will pull a very wide selection of free themes into your work area:

You can sort these themes by Featured – Popular – Latest – and Feature Filter:

Note too that we can upload themes. That's usually used when you buy from a 3rd party.

Featured – Popular – Latest are all self-explanatory. I want to talk you through the Feature Filter as this is where I would head first.

Things to Look for in a Theme

When you select a free theme, here are some things to look for:

Is it a responsive design?

This is an absolute 'must' nowadays; you should not even consider any design unless it is fully mobile responsive.

Is it regularly updated and properly supported?

Everything costs something to provide, and I personally believe that paid is best and developers have a right to make a living.

So, if a developer creates a theme for free – more as a hobby than a job – you may have to wait until he or she gets around to updating it if it breaks.

Look for a well-supported, well-used theme which has a back history of updates.

If you don't do this, you may find that you're looking for a new blog theme sooner rather than later.

Does the theme get great reviews?

Themes get starred reviews, as you would on eBay or Amazon. Look for a theme with lots of positive reviews.

A great thing to look for is if a theme has a paid for and a free version.

This means that – to put it bluntly – the freebie is the bait to get you to upgrade.

That's good, though because it means that the free version will be well-supported.

How to Select Your Theme

Click on the Feature Filter link, and you'll be taken to a page of options:

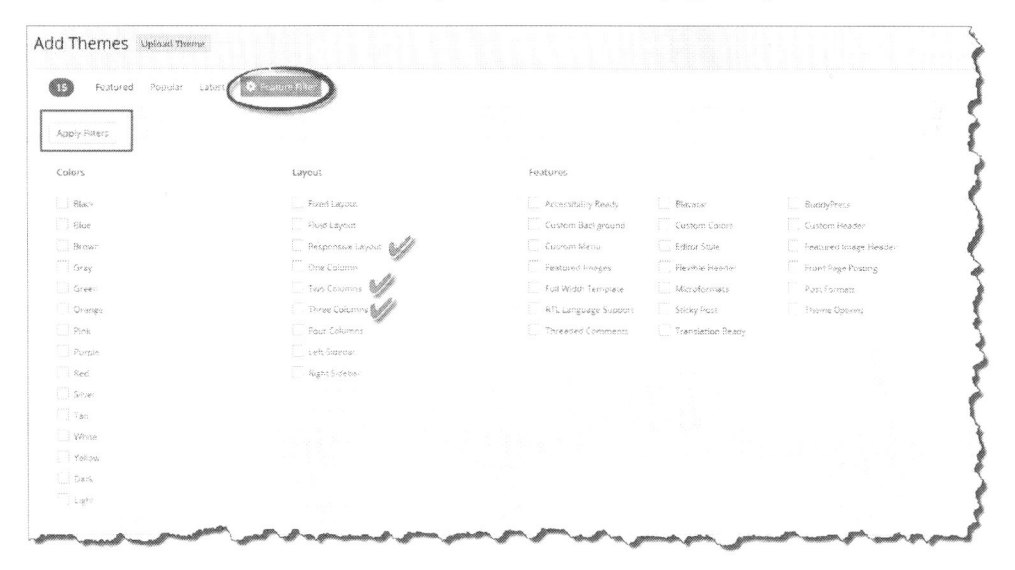

Much of this page is personal preference.

For instance, it's up to you what colour you like; I don't have an opinion on that, it's a matter of personal taste.

However, there are some key settings which I do recommend.

I think that responsive design is non-negotiable if you want your readers to be able to access you on all devices, so make sure that you have this selected.

Sites which are not responsive on mobile devices will shortly be going the same way as the Yellow Pages.

I also prefer two column and three column designs as a rule.

One column looks ridiculous, four columns look too cluttered, but that's just my opinion.

I recommend looking at two and three columns.

The rest is a matter of choice.

As a beginner, have a good look around and see what's out there.

Just click **Apply Filters** to restrict the type of theme that you're offered.

Otherwise, it's like looking for the proverbial needle in a haystack.

There is a **Search Themes** option too (see 1 below) – just insert keywords and see what comes up – and a rather bizarre and somewhat limited **Subject** option too.

Use personal preferences for these. I would generally search just for two and three column responsive themes and take it from there.

When selecting themes, I really encourage you to do so with an attitude of openness and experimentation.

Try stuff and if you don't like it - change it - and keep going until you're happy.

It's only when you start paying that you have to be more careful with your choices.

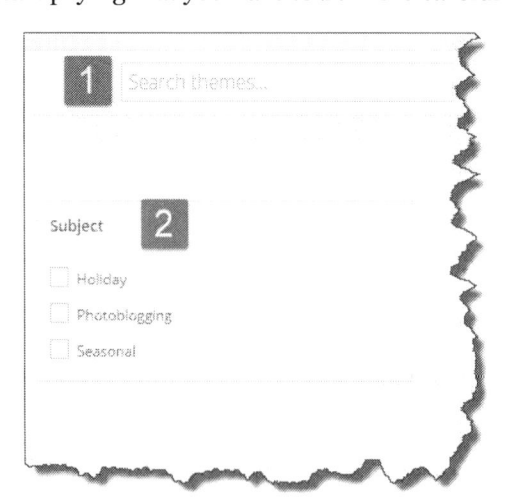

How to Change Your Theme

Wordpress has made theme surfing much easier in recent updates, with the inclusion of that useful **Preview** button.

Just hold your cursor over any theme, and two button options appear in the bottom right-hand corner, labelled **Install** and **Preview**.

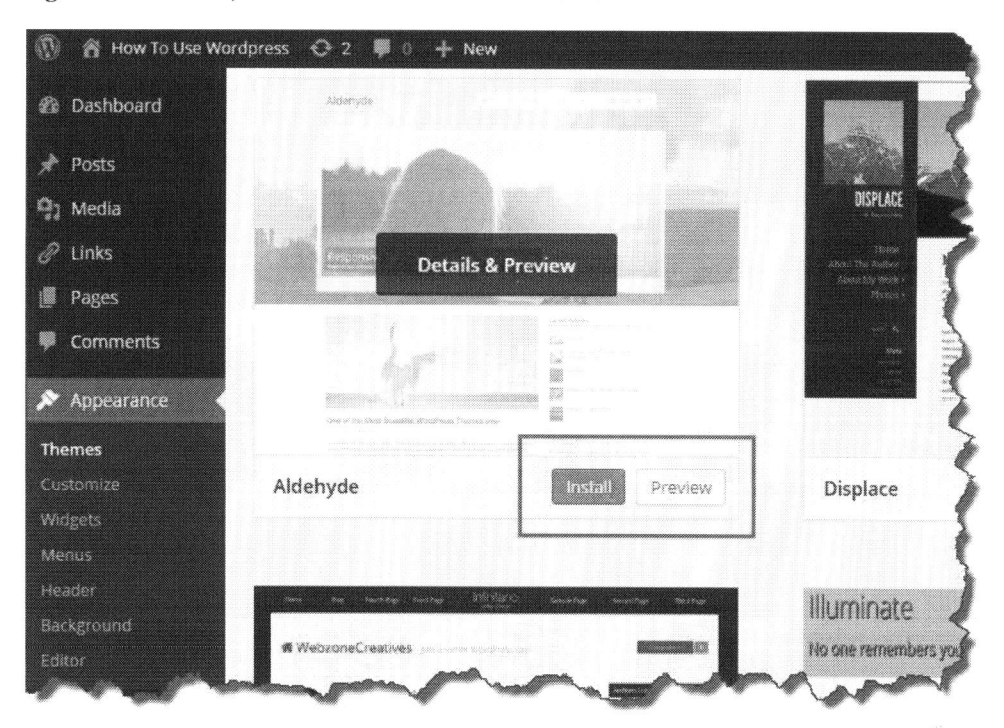

If you click on **Preview**, you get a really good feel for how the theme will look when installed.

In a later step, once you have actually installed the theme, Wordpress will allow you to live preview with the content that you have already created, without you having to actually activate anything.

That's a really useful function to access if you have a busy and active blog and you can't afford to make a make a mess of things.

In the meantime, if you like the look of a theme, just install it.

It's useful to note that it doesn't actually activate the theme at this step, it just makes it available to you in your themes library on your blog.

Note the reviews and versions information in the preview pages; this is how you assess the quality of a theme and the level of technical support that it's likely to get:

To select any theme, just click the blue **Install** button.

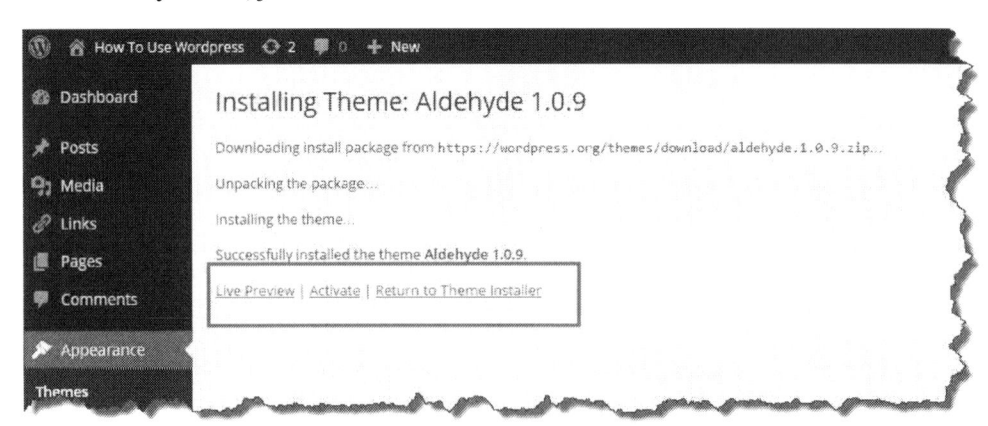

You now get three choices.

Live Preview will let you view your blog content in the new theme, without changing anything (yet) for your readers.

Activate will remove the existing theme and install the new theme.

Return to Theme Installer will let you carry on hunting for new themes.

I would encourage you to install the themes that you like – as many as you please – at this stage, so that you can preview exactly how they'd look alongside your own content.

Just line them all up, and we can delete them later.

Or just leave them in your personal Theme Library area for later. It's entirely up to you.

I like to keep my blog as lean and clean as possible, so I do tend to have a habit of clearing things out which I have no intention of using.

You're usually given a few customization options with each theme. Play around with these and see what they do.

If you need, say, a decent header image or background image and you don't know how to make one, let me recommend fiverr at https://www.fiverr.com/.

For $5 and upwards you can get virtually any job that you can think of done by a remote worker.

I use this service very frequently, whenever I hit a roadblock with my own skills, and it's well worth getting acquainted with.

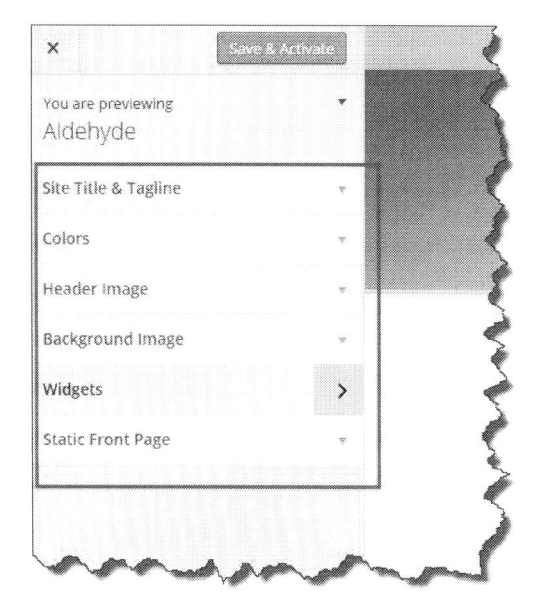

Once you click that **Save & Activate** button, your theme is installed.

From there it's just a case of 'rinse and repeat.'

Remove themes, add themes, delete themes - there's no limit at all.

The one thing I would recommend though is doing your experimentation *before* you have readers. If you keep messing about with your blog, people will lose patience.

So experiment as much as you want to at the beginning, but once you generate a readership, you need to keep things consistent.

Just think about how you feel when you go into a supermarket, and they have moved all the shelves around.

That's how your regular readers will feel if you change things too much, so once things are underway with your blogging, only change your theme when the old one has become unfit for purpose.

There's just one more thing to mention with themes, and that's how to permanently delete them.

You cannot delete a live theme; it must be deactivated and replaced with another theme first.

To delete any inactive theme, hold your cursor over its preview image to display the **Theme Details** button:

You'll get the theme details as promised, and the **Delete** button is tucked away right at the bottom on the right-hand side.

It used to be much more straightforward to delete a theme directly, but that is one thing that, at the time of writing this book, recently took a small step backwards in my opinion.

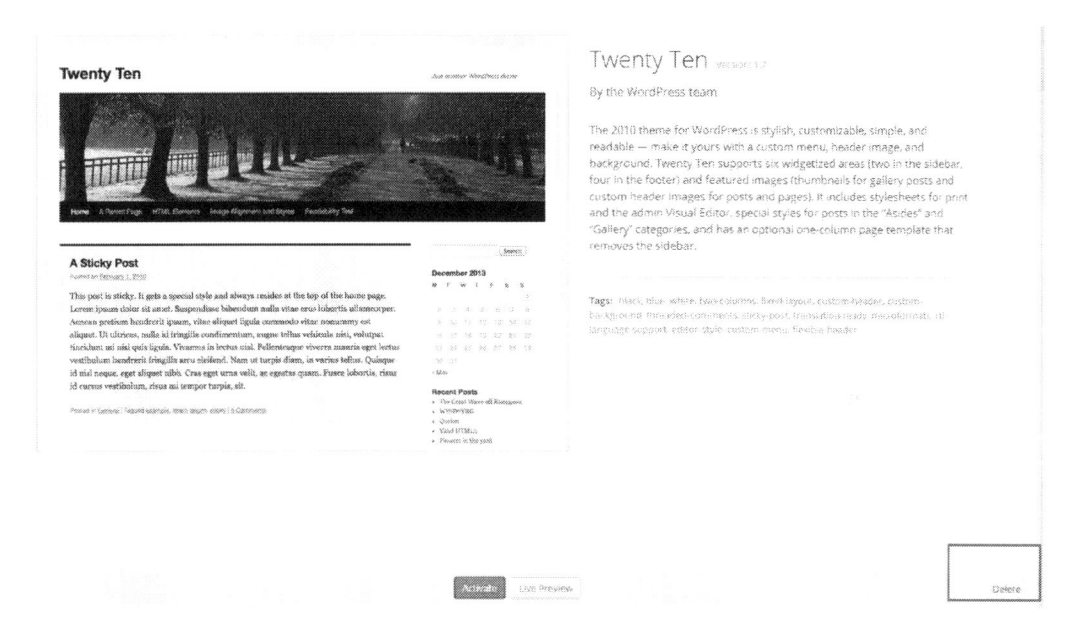

You now know how to search for, install, replace and delete free themes.

As a final note, if you prefer, you can search themes directly from within the main directory: https://wordpress.org/themes/

The Best Providers of Paid Themes

You already know how much I love Optimizepress and Thrive Themes but before I made the complete switch to those products I used paid for themes from a number of excellent sources.

Most WordPress themes provide:

- The overall look and style of your blog

- A range of font options

- A range of colour options

- A range of widget locations

- A mix of styles for posts

- A range of page layouts

- A mix of additional stylistic settings

Put simply, paid for themes give you more options, better support, and more reliable performance.

They are often optimized for SEO too, and I can't believe that anybody is still selling non-responsive themes anymore ... though I could be wrong!

Here are my favourite paid theme providers. I have purchased from all of them in the past:

iThemes: Take a look at https://ithemes.com/

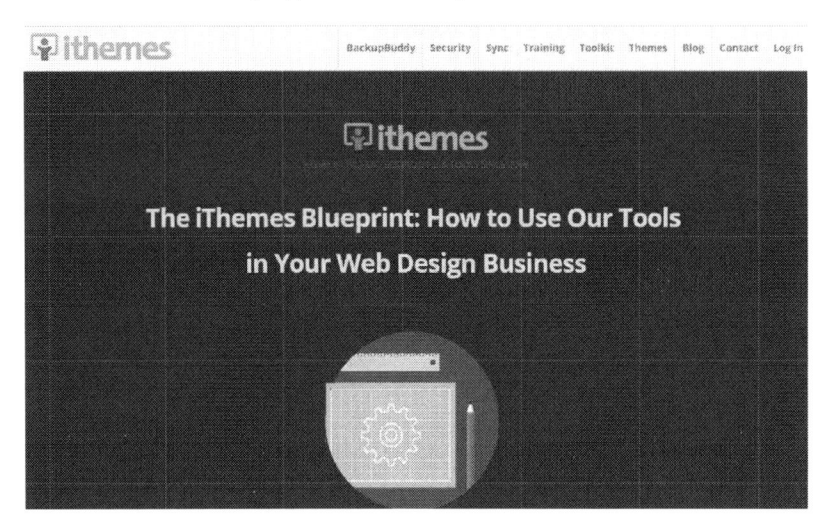

Woo Commerce: Take a look at https://www.woothemes.com/

Note: A 'must-see' if you want to set up a shop on your blog, Woo Themes is very widely used to take payments, manage customers and list products on Wordpress sites.

It has a very good reputation and good support. I have used it myself in the past.

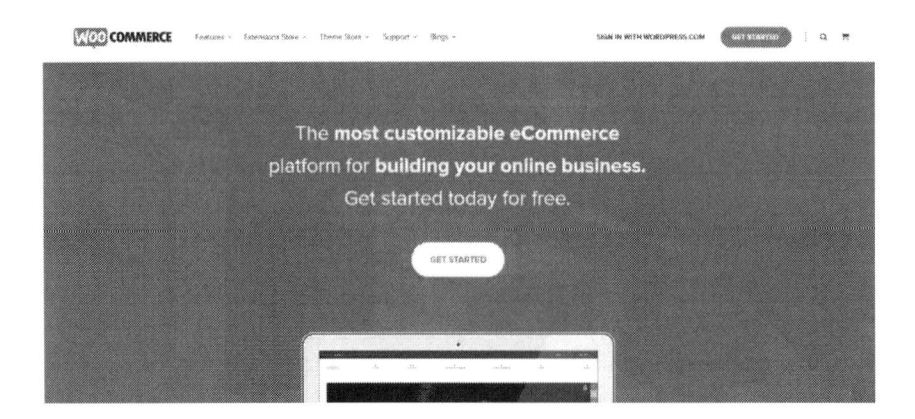

ThemeForest: Take a look at https://themeforest.net/

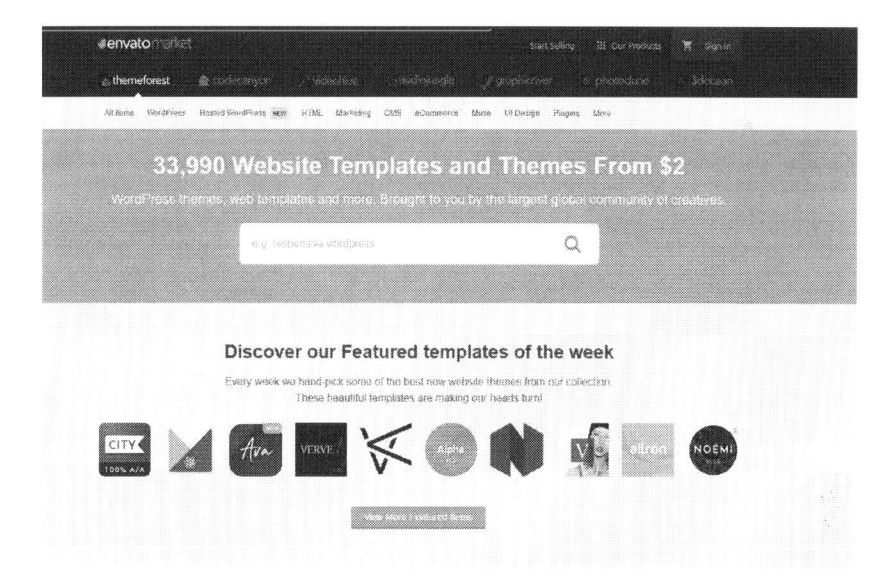

There's not a lot to say about the specific sites, other than they offer a great selection of options, but if you are looking for a high quality, reasonably priced theme with great support, you can browse and buy in confidence with any one of those three services.

I've bought most themes via Themeforest which is my particular favourite, but if you need to build a shop on your blog, or you want to take payments easily, Woo Themes is the place to go.

Chapter 9: Wordpress Plugins

What is a Plugin?

This is how Wordpress describes plugins:

Plugins can extend WordPress to do almost anything you can imagine. In the directory you can find, download, rate, and comment on all the best plugins the WordPress community has to offer.

In short, plugins allow you to do amazing things on your blog with zero technical skills required.

Speaking as somebody who had to learn to code in 2001 to be able to make websites, when I look at what Wordpress gives us for free, I'm astounded.

Plugins are amazing. There's a huge free directory of them, and if you start to pay for them, you'll discover that they can do much more incredible things.

I'll give you a selection free and essential plugins in the next chapter, but I have many more installed across all of my sites.

We'll save that for a more advanced book on Wordpress, though. For now, let's see what they can do.

A Word About Free and Paid Plugins

What I said about free and paid themes applies to free and paid plugins.

Paid plugins have better support, they usually perform better when Wordpress rolls out an update, and they provide greater functionality.

However, there are many excellent free plugins (I'll be recommending several in the next chapter!) which have excellent support and consistent performance.

With plugins, the following checks apply:

<u>Does it do something that you *need* on your blog?</u>

The sure sign of a web amateur is somebody who adds all the free stuff to their site – just because they can.

In these days of mobile devices, less is more.

Go for lean, clean and easy to navigate at all times.

So ask yourself, do you really need that plugin, or are you just adding it to your blog because it does something really cool?

<u>Is it regularly updated and properly supported?</u>

Look for a well-supported, well-used plugin which has a back history of updates.

If you don't do this, you may find that your blog has problems further down the line.

Always seek quality plugins which have widespread usage and a good track record.

<u>Does the plugin get great reviews?</u>

Plugins get starred reviews too, so look for a one with lots of positive reviews.

A great thing to look for – as with themes - is if a plugin has a paid for and a free version.

This means that the free version will be well supported, after all, nobody is going to upgrade if the free trial is rubbish.

Where to Find Free Plugins

You can search for plugins directly from within the main directory if you want to: https://wordpress.org/plugins/

However, I search for and install my plugins directly from within my blog.

When you get to the plugins page, if you have followed this book step-by-step you will see Akismet already installed by default.

Akismet helps to prevent comment spam which is a big problem on most blogs, so we are going to use this plugin.

I'll talk more about it in the next chapter, but for now, you may find that Akismet needs to be updated:

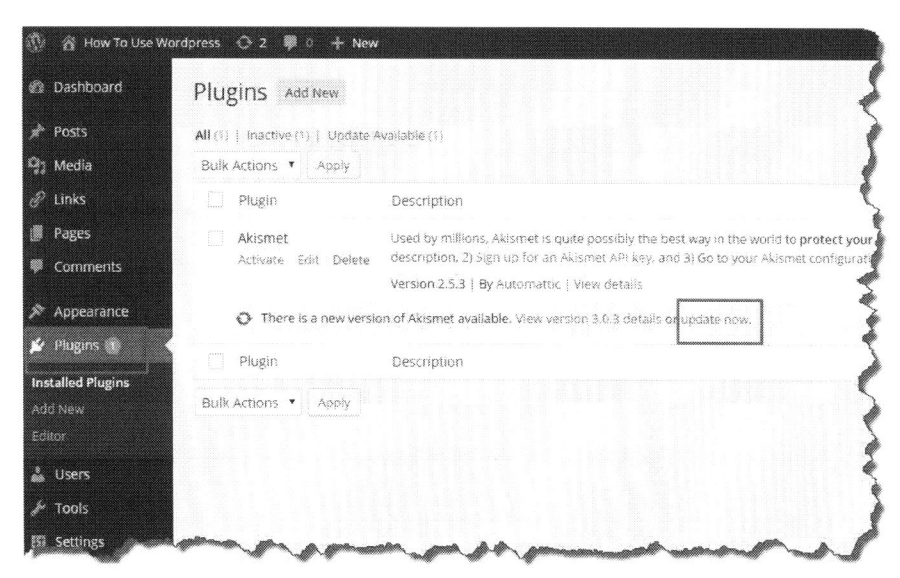

If it does, just click the **update now** link and wait until Wordpress confirms completion with the next screen:

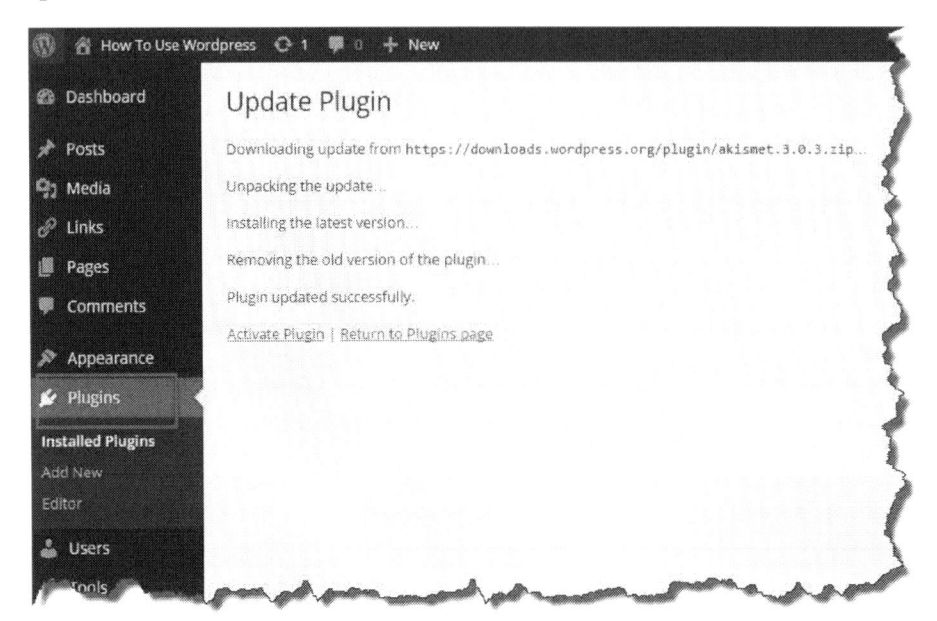

For now, just go back to **Plugins** via the menu. We'll activate Akismet in the next chapter as it's not as straightforward as just clicking a button.

Click the **Add New** button now to take us to the main plugins area:

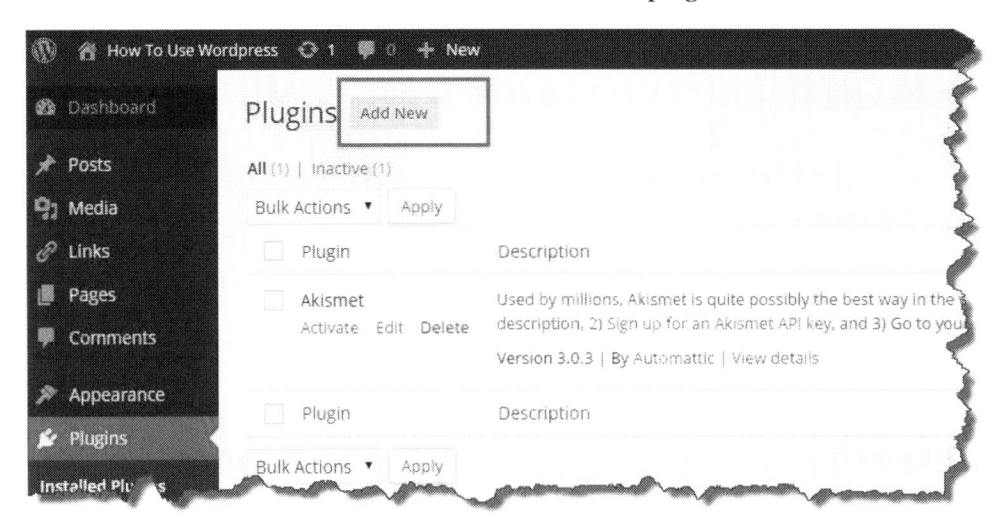

The plugins area is quite a busy section, but it's very easy to navigate:

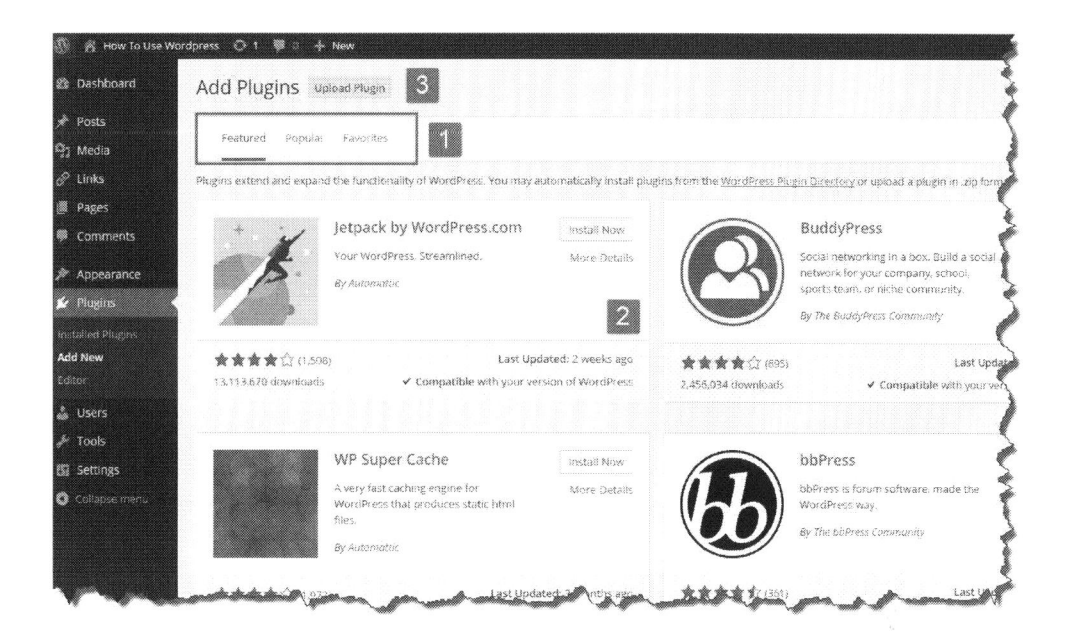

We can view Featured – Popular – Favorites in the plugins area (see 1 in the image above), and this works just the same as themes. It helps you to get to the more relevant plugins.

Jetpack is a very popular plugin (see 2 in the image above) and if you were sitting in a 1-to-1 beginner's class with me, I'd probably encourage you to install it as a 'fix all.'

However, I'm assuming that if you're still reading this book, you're deadly serious about creating a proper Wordpress blog and – without being geeky or snobby about it – there are better options available than Jetpack.

It's great - please don't get me wrong on this - but as a serious Wordpress user, I just don't need it.

I would install Jetpack for people who absolutely hate any kind of online work and who have no intention whatsoever of getting 'under the bonnet.'

Finally, we can **Upload Plugin** (see 3 in the image above), but we never have to do this for free plugins.

This operation can wait until I write an 'Advanced' version of this book, as we'll only use it with paid plugins (with just a few exceptions which don't apply here).

Note on the far right-hand side of that screen we also get the option to **Search Plugins**:

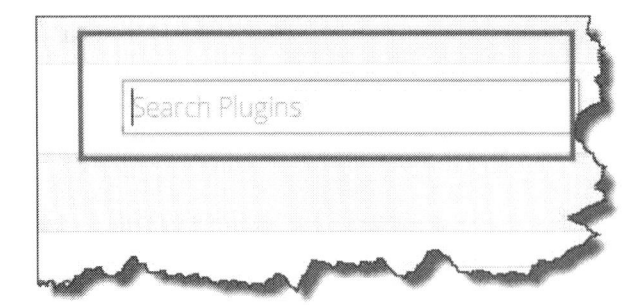

This is where we'll be heading next.

How to Install a Plugin

Let's install our first plugin

For your first plugin, we're going to install one that requires no additional set up at all.

We just 'set and forget.'

When we get to the next chapter, I'll show you the next step in plugin installation, whereby you install them, then you have to adjust some settings to configure them properly.

If you remember in the Media chapter, I mentioned a rather annoying problem in Wordpress whereby images have superfluous links added to them by default.

Well, we're going to solve that problem right now so it never bothers us again, using a free plugin.

Head for **Search Plugins** and enter the text **no image link** and press your **Return** key on your keyboard:

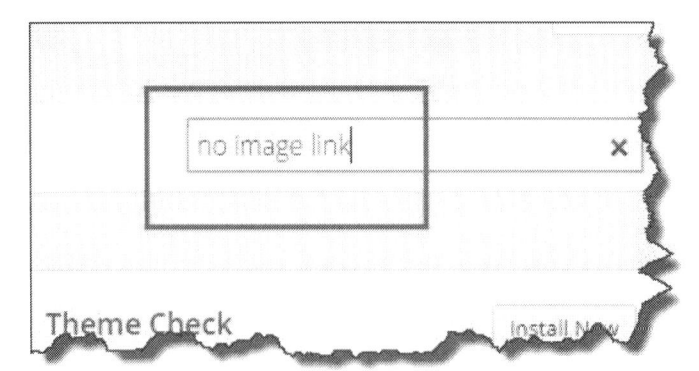

This will return a number of options, but the first of those is the plugin **No Image Link** by Scott Werner, and that's the one that we're after.

121

Notice the five-star reviews, the 5359 downloads and the **Compatible with your version of Wordpress** message.

That's the sign of a good, free plugin.

Also, pay attention to the **Last Updated** information.

If the plugin hasn't been updated for a long time, that's probably not a good sign, and you're best looking for an alternative unless it's recommended by a trusted source and is a plugin which perhaps does not require regular updating.

Click on the **Install Now** button:

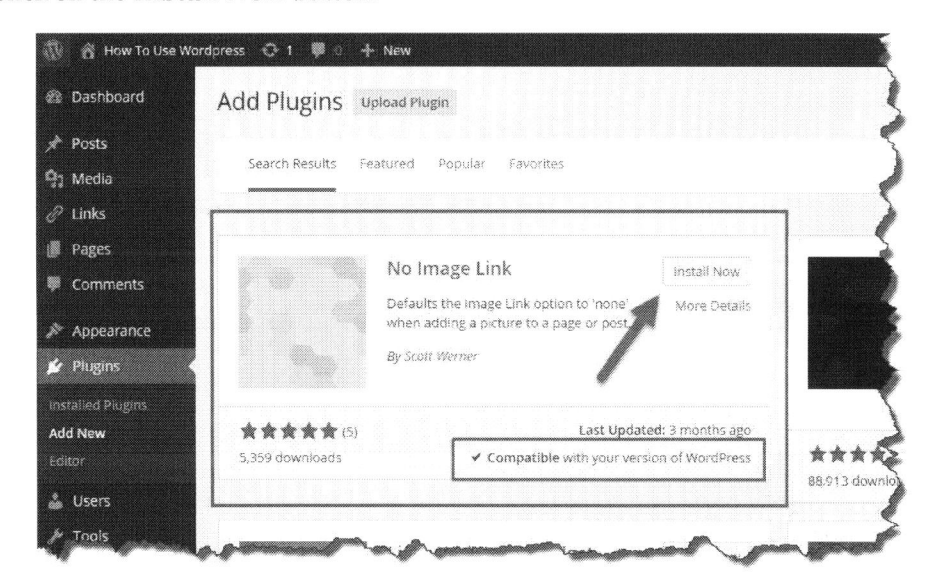

Wordpress installs the plugin – never interrupt this process – and we get a confirmation message:

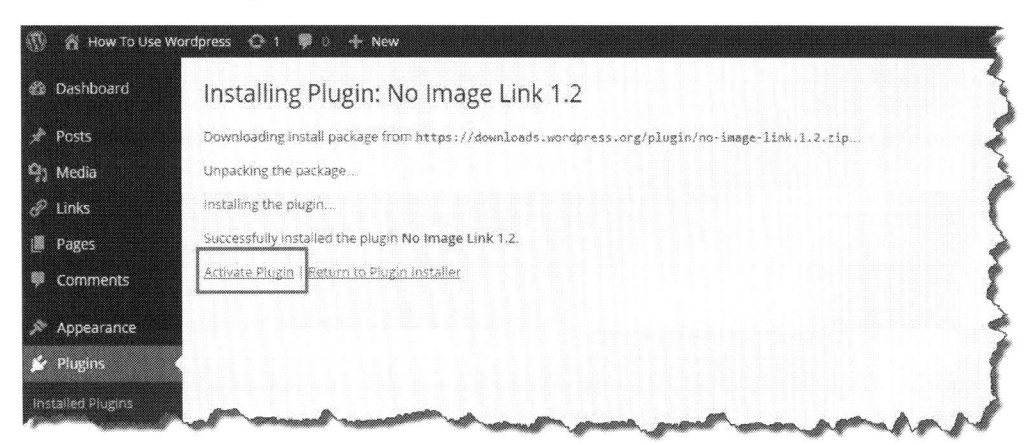

Click on **Activate Plugin** and the process is completed. The plugin is doing its job already.

Note how we can have plugins installed and not activated (see 1 in the image below) and installed and activated (see 2 in the image below).

We can activate and deactivate them just by clicking on the appropriate link.

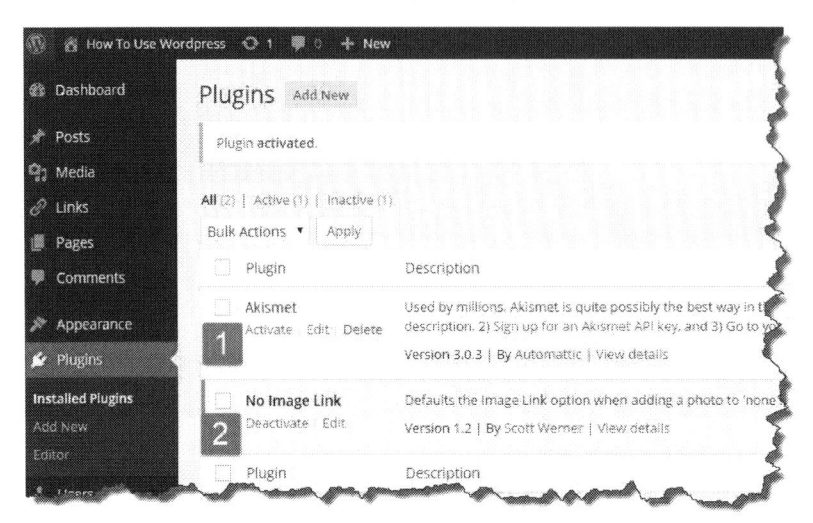

To check that **No Image Link** is working correctly, I can now open up a new post and try to insert an image:

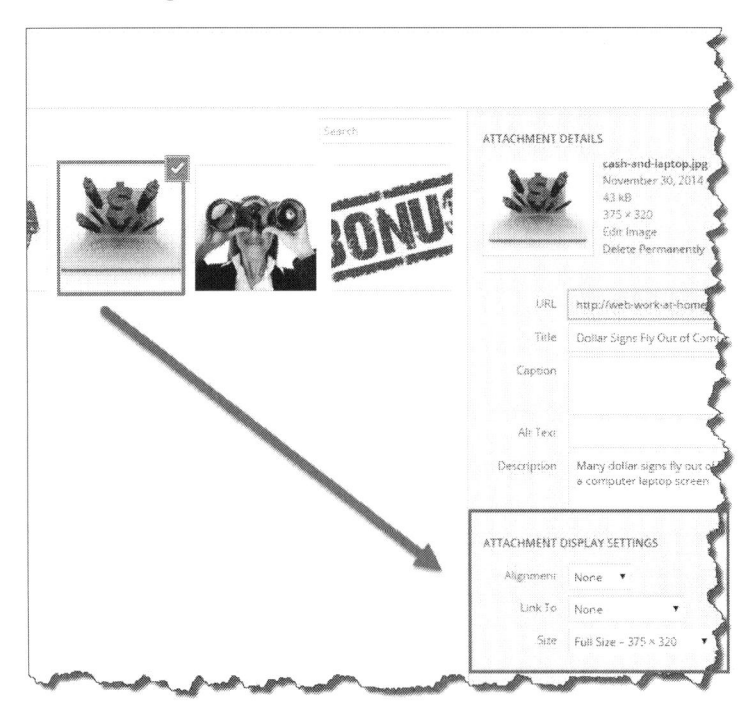

You can see that Wordpress is no longer generating that horrible link. It defaults to **None** (exactly how we want it!) and will continue to do so unless we deactivate or delete that **No Image Link** plugin.

Installing plugins is as easy as that!

Years ago that would have been a major coding project, but these days we just search – click – install and we're done.

How to remove a Plugin

Remember that you can deactivate a plugin rather than delete it, but at times you will want to delete one.

This usually happens if you install a rogue plugin which interferes with other plugins on your blog.

Only occasionally, with some plugins, you're pleased to see the back of them.

Deletion is easy, but please note that as with themes, you cannot delete an active plugin. You must deactivate it first.

To do that, just click the deactivate link in the menu below the name of the plugin.

In this example, we have not yet activated Akismet so we could delete it if we wanted to - we would just click on that **Delete** link:

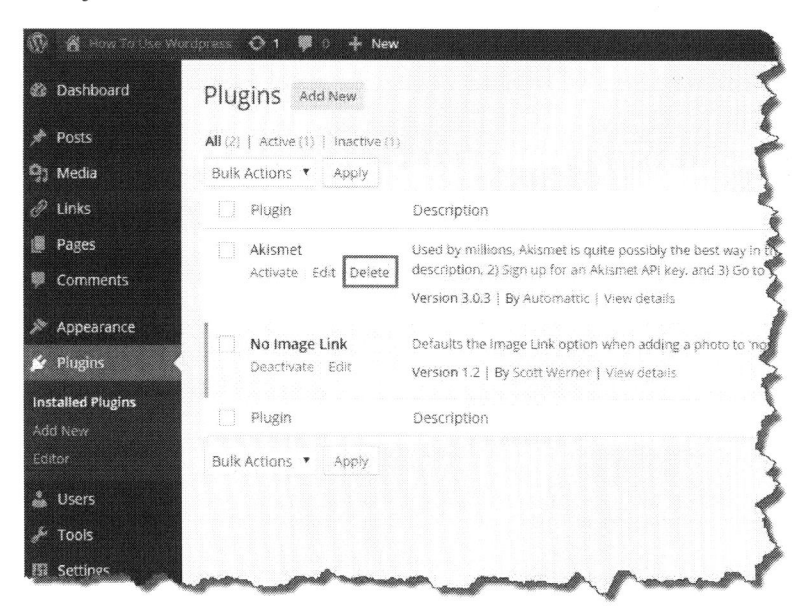

Remember, if deleting a number of plugins at one sitting, we could use the **Bulk Actions** menu – we'd just check the boxes of the plugins that we wanted to get rid of, then delete them all at once, rather than one at a time.

Once you click the **Delete** link, you'll be asked to confirm:

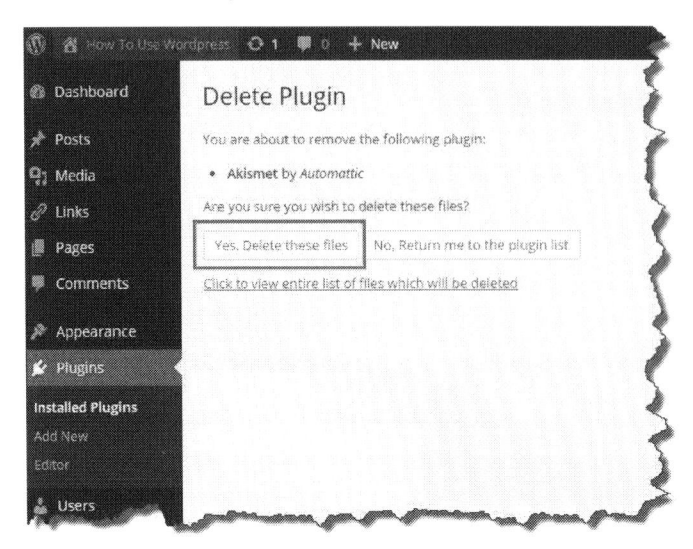

Simply click on **Yes, Delete these files,** and the plugin is gone.

If ever you change your mind again in the future, just install it once again by searching for the plugin as we did at the beginning of this chapter.

Bulk Plugin Operations

There is a second way to update, activate, deactivate and delete plugins, and we usually do it this way if there is more than one plugin involved, i.e., updating or deleting 2+ plugins at one time.

In this case, we check the boxes next to the individual plugins, or select all of the available plugins, and click the **Bulk Actions** drop-down menu:

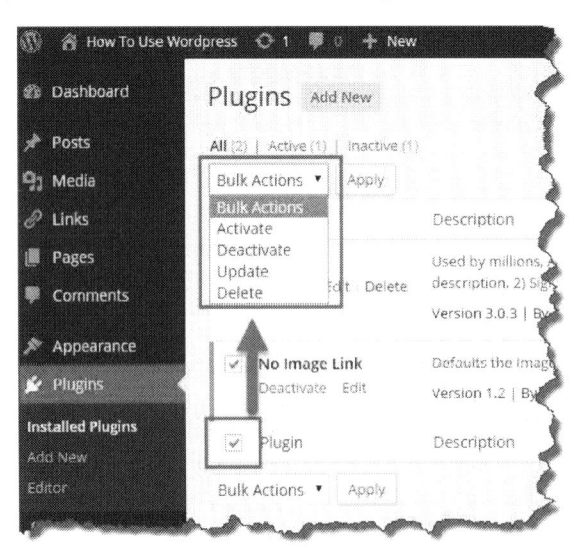

We can then Activate, Deactivate, Update or Delete several plugins at one time.

Just remember to click the **Apply** button to complete the operation.

Now you know all about the basics of plugins use, we can install some great free tools and power up your blog.

By the way, because I have so many Wordpress sites, I use a great service called ManageWP at http://managewp.com/ which allows me to access all of my blogs via a single dashboard and update the plugs and themes all at once.

It's a real timesaver and an essential tool if you ever end up with more than one Wordpress site.

Chapter 10: Essential Wordpress Plugins

Having got to grips with the powerhouse of Wordpress (i.e., plugins!), we can now pick off some of the essential tools that any Wordpress installation needs.

Before we do so, the basic plugin selection that I am recommending is based on my own experience over several years.

I use these plugins, I like them, and I know other online marketers who use them successfully though other bloggers will also have their own favourites too.

There may well be better plugins out there, and I certainly have many more installed on my own blog, but this basic list has been selected on the basis that they perform essential jobs which need to be done if you're going to be a successful blogger.

They are also 'beginner friendly; I didn't want to make things too complicated at this stage.

So, in summary, I've gone more complicated than Jetpack – which is too basic for serious bloggers – and I've gone less complicated than a professional blogger would go.

But these will set you up very nicely and see you on your way to your successful blogging career.

I am assuming in this section that you have read the last chapter and that you know how to search for a plugin by name, install and activate it.

All of these plugins will be found by using the **Search Plugins** option. Just search for them by their names as they appear below:

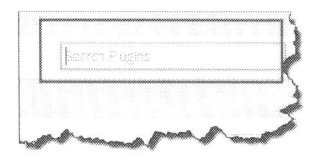

f these plugins require some additional configuration. Where that is the case I .ven you my tips to help you set them up fast without having to wade through the manual.

Essential Plugin: XML Sitemaps

Take a look at https://wordpress.org/plugins/google-sitemap-generator/

Full instructions at https://wordpress.org/plugins/google-sitemap-generator/installation/

Why you need it in a nutshell:

Search Engine Optimization!

This plugin automatically builds a sitemap which tells the search engines all about your lovely content.

That means they can find everything that you create and it makes it much easier for people online to find your blog.

My tips:

Just install it and activate.

The first time you publish a post, it will begin to work its magic.

Blogs take a while to get found and indexed by search engines – it takes months sometimes – but using a tool like this, you'll reduce that time considerably.

Essential Plugin: Anti-spam

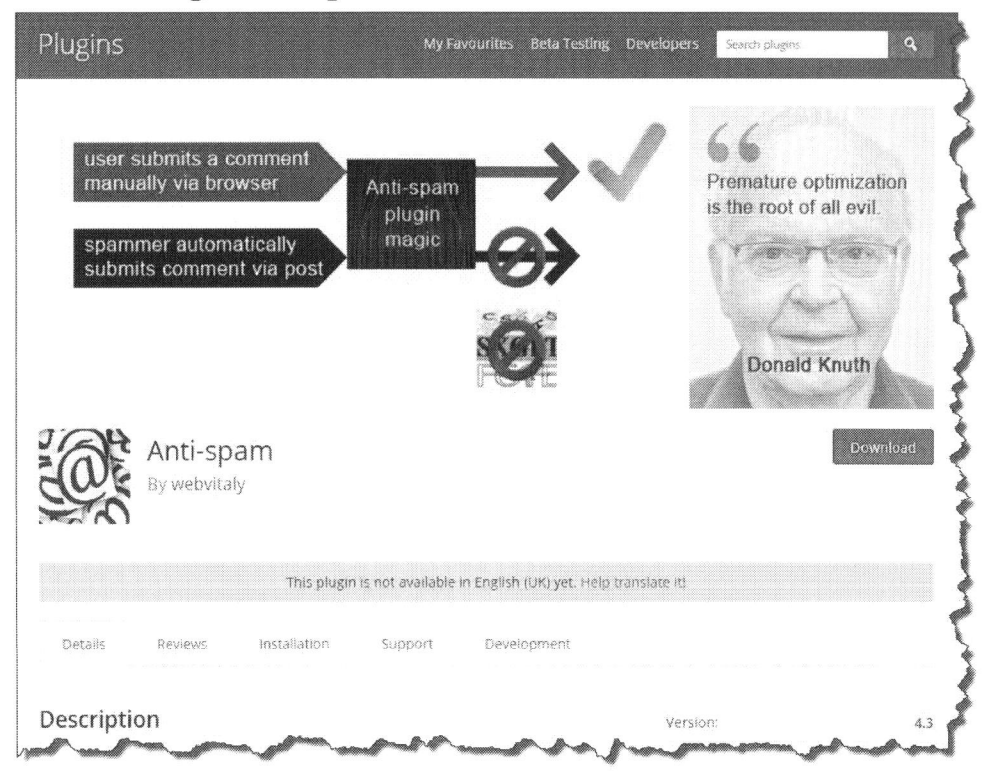

Take a look at https://en-gb.wordpress.org/plugins/anti-spam/

Full instructions at https://en-gb.wordpress.org/plugins/anti-spam/#installation

Why you need it in a nutshell:

When you write a blog, you will get blogging spam.

And lots of it!

Akismet is the plugin that is installed by default, and it is excellent, but you're supposed to pay for it for commercial use.

A great and free alternative is Anti-spam which I have used very happily since they started charging for Akismet.

It automatically intercepts this spam and makes your life sweet and easy.

Akismet uses an API key; you probably won't like that very much if you're new to Wordpress.

So stick with Anti-spam, it does a great job and will cost you nothing.

Essential Plugin: All in One SEO Pack

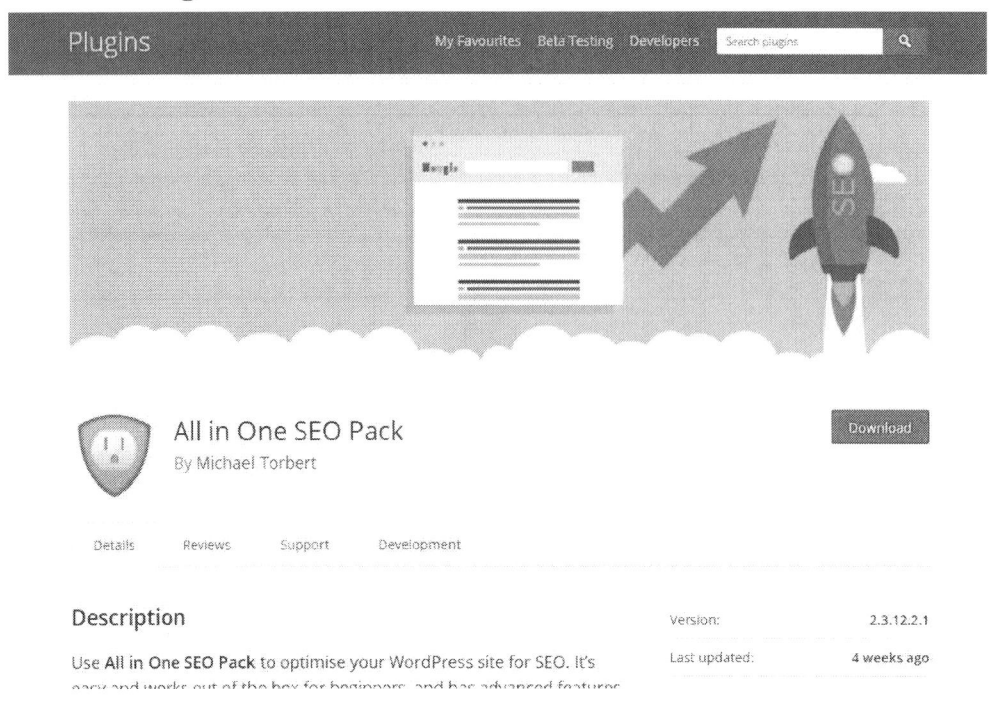

Take a look at https://wordpress.org/plugins/all-in-one-seo-pack/

Full instructions at https://wordpress.org/plugins/all-in-one-seo-pack/installation/

Why you need it in a nutshell:

More search engine optimization.

In short, using a tool like this will get your blog posts found.

Many people use Yoast at https://yoast.com/wordpress/plugins/seo/.

Personally, I always got on better with All in One SEO Pack

My tips:

To change the settings, go to the plugins area and click on **Options configuration panel**:

This will take you to an options page on which there is quite a lot of nasty SEO terminology.

This book is for beginners, so let's keep it really simple.

Leave all the defaults as they are, but make sure that you customize the Home Page Settings area with your own Home Title, Home Description and Home Keywords.

Also, make sure that **Use Keywords** is enabled.

Thereafter, whenever you create a new post or page, you'll get an area at the bottom where you can add in your basic SEO information.

Do this every time; it will help your posts and pages to get found in the search engines:

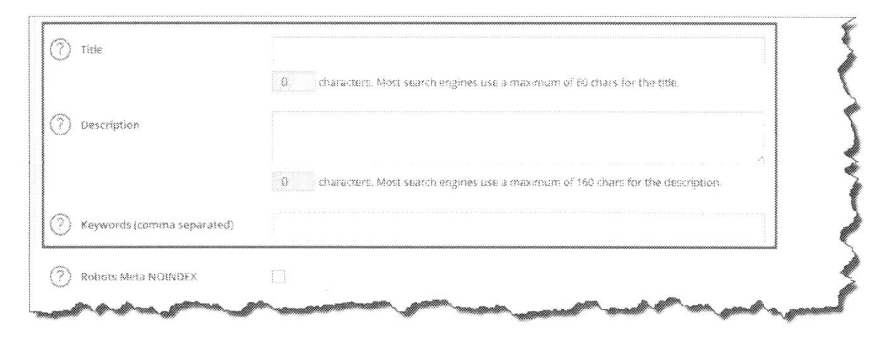

Now, there's a lot more to that particular plugin, but that will get you started very nicely for now.

UpDraft Plus Backup and Restoration

Take a look at https://wordpress.org/plugins/updraftplus/

Full instructions at https://wordpress.org/plugins/updraftplus/installation/

Why you need it in a nutshell:

It's really important to backup your Wordpress blog in case you get hacked or ever, in error, mess it all up.

I've struggled to find a backup plugin that I like in the past, but a geek colleague recommended this to me recently, and I instantly loved it:

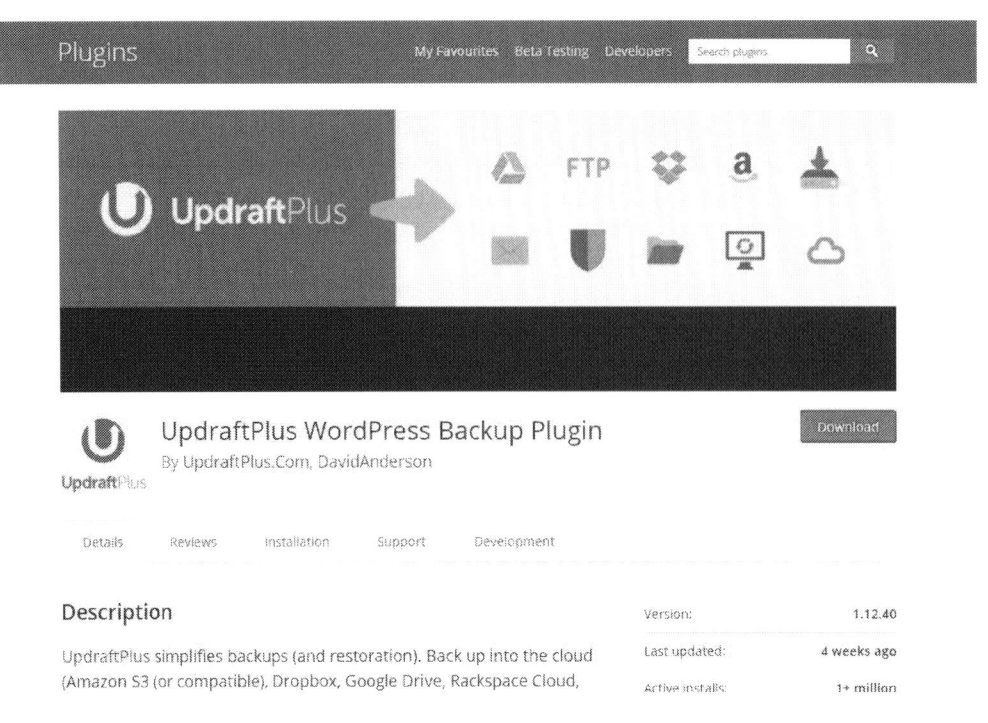

My tips:

This is a great plugin to use because it makes life so simple.

In the past the backup plugins that I used were slow and cumbersome. This one is fast, self-explanatory and reliable, with straightforward one-click backup (1), Restore from backup (2), Cloning and migration (3) which is very useful if you ever change web host, and simple storage and access to backed-up files (4):

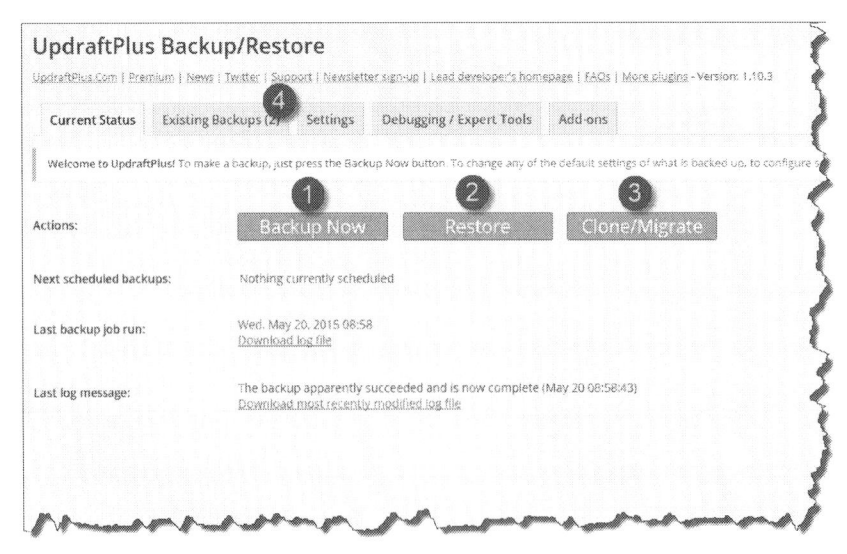

Essential Plugin: Cookie Law Info

Take a look at https://wordpress.org/plugins/cookie-law-info/

Full instructions at https://wordpress.org/plugins/cookie-law-info/installation/

Why you need it in a nutshell:

If you're in the EU and you intend to advertise or track visitors in any way, you need to display this.

If you're not in the EU, I suggest you just play safe and use it anyway.

My tips:

Just install and activate this plugin, and it will pop up a notification strip at the bottom of your blog:

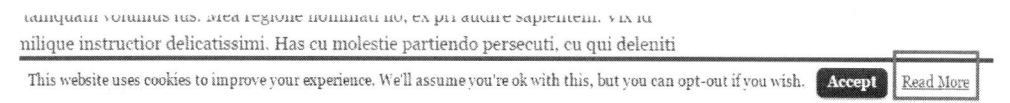

There is one adjustment that we have to make - that Read More link doesn't lead anywhere just yet.

It will just link directly back to your main website URL at the moment.

Navigate to the Cookie Law plugin settings link and click it:

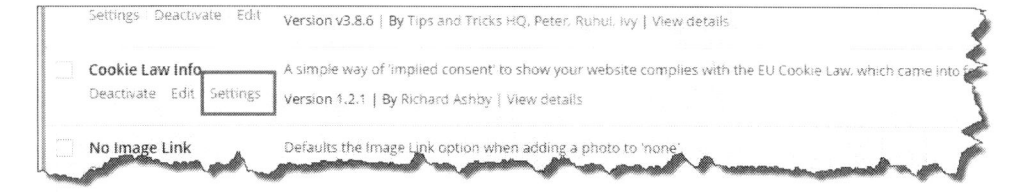

On the settings page, scroll down to the menu area:

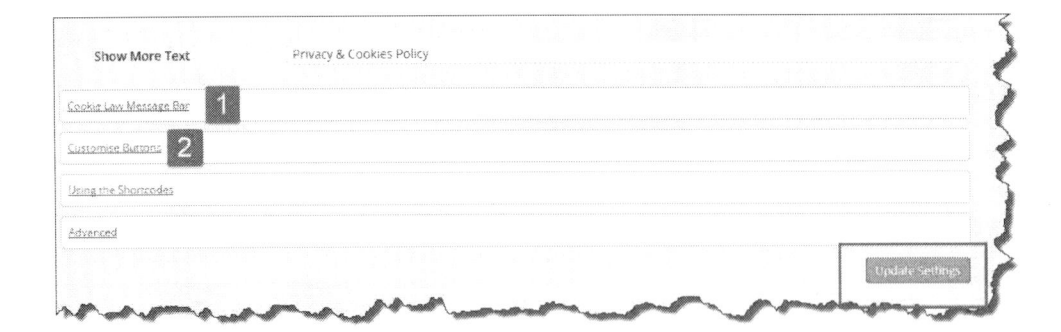

You have two options; you can just remove that Read More link altogether by clicking on **Cookie Law Message Bar** in the menu options (1 in the image above):

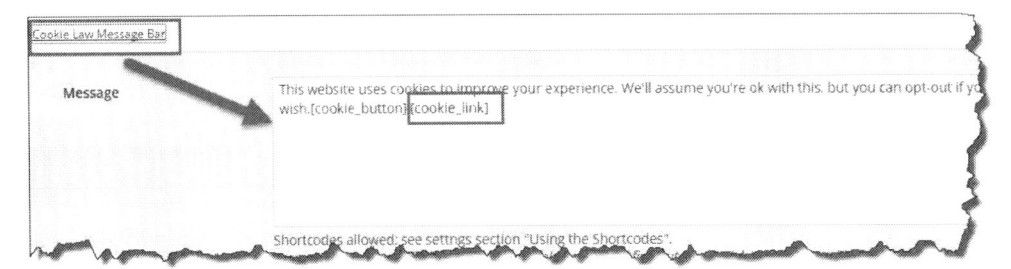

Alternatively, you can insert a link to your privacy page (if you have one!) by clicking on **Customise Buttons** in the menu options (2 in the image above):

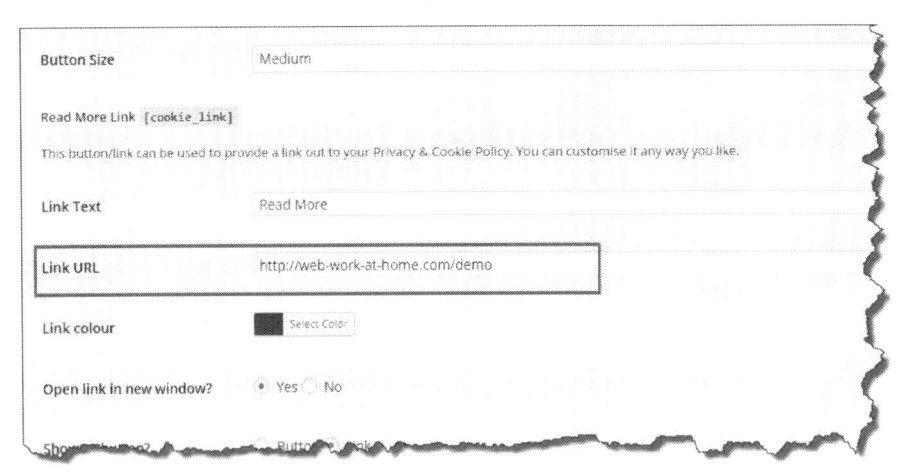

Either way, you've got yourself a nice, unobtrusive privacy notice to keep you EU law compliant.

If you're not in the EU, it's good practice anyway to display your privacy policy, so this is a still a useful tool.

Essential Plugin: Social Media Share Buttons and Social Icons (Ultimate Sharing)

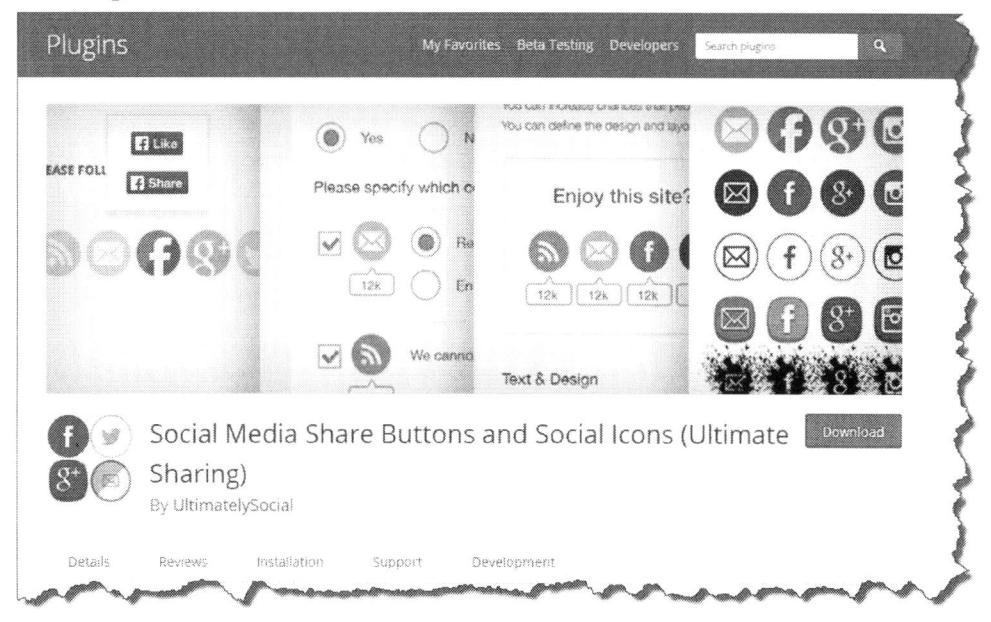

Take a look at https://wordpress.org/plugins/ultimate-social-media-icons/

Full instructions at https://wordpress.org/plugins/ultimate-social-media-icons/#installation

Why you need it in a nutshell:

Social media sharing!

This is a great thing to have on your site; it means that readers can easily share your content, thus bringing in even more readers.

There are many social button options, but this looks really nice and is easy to use.

My tips:

Don't feel like you have to enable every social media platform, but you should certainly use the ones that you're active on.

I like this plugin because it gives you multiple social media icon options, so you can select the look and feel which suits your site best.

I generally like my social media icons at the end of a post, but you may also wish to experiment with the 'floating' option, which places icons to the side of each post.

I would certainly recommend that you work through all of the options (1-8) shown in the image on the next page and complete the info as fully as you can:

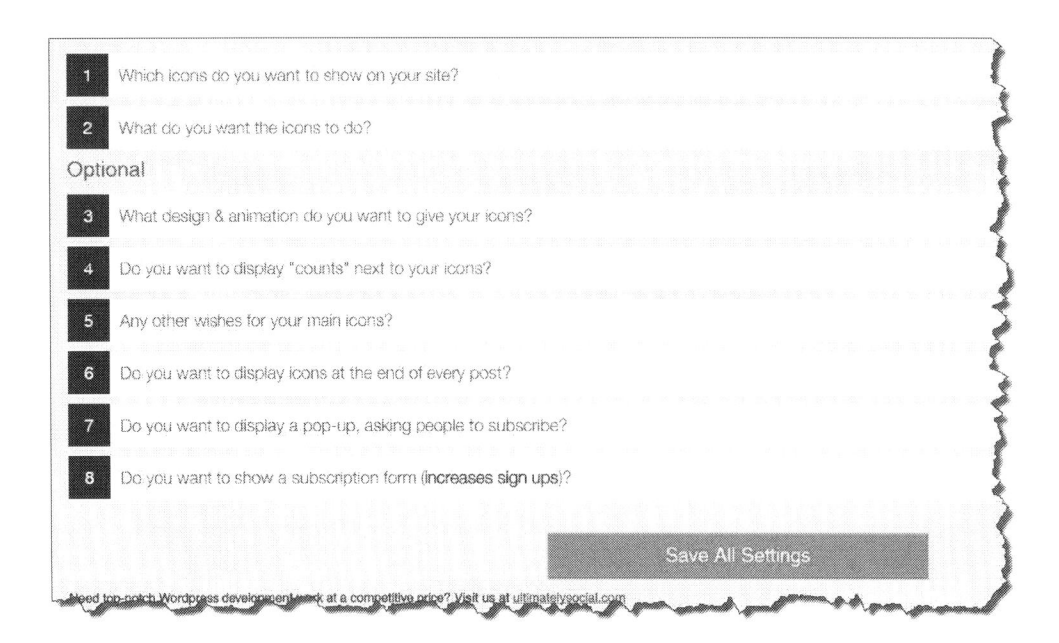

| 1 | Which icons do you want to show on your site? |
| 2 | What do you want the icons to do? |

Optional

3	What design & animation do you want to give your icons?
4	Do you want to display "counts" next to your icons?
5	Any other wishes for your main icons?
6	Do you want to display icons at the end of every post?
7	Do you want to display a pop-up, asking people to subscribe?
8	Do you want to show a subscription form (**increases sign ups**)?

Save All Settings

In use, it creates a neat and highly visual set of social buttons which mean that your content can be shared socially across multiple sites.

That's a good thing for any new blogger.

Essential Plugin: All in One WP Security & Firewall

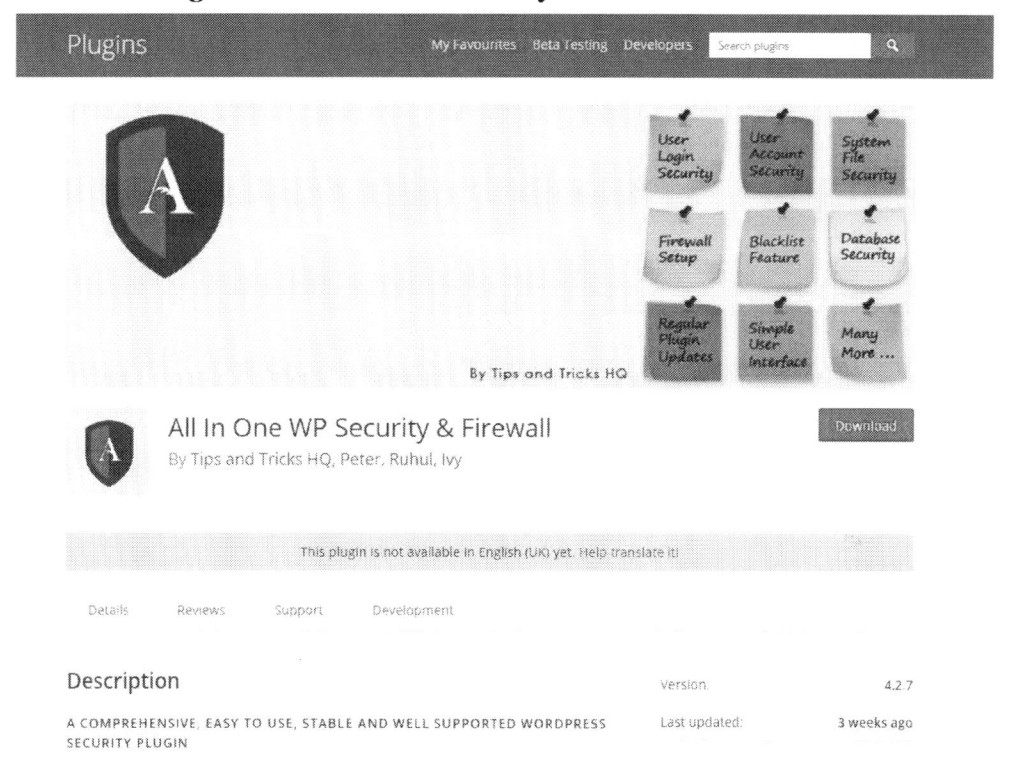

Take a look at https://wordpress.org/plugins/all-in-one-wp-security-and-firewall/

Full instructions at https://wordpress.org/plugins/all-in-one-wp-security-and-firewall/installation/

Why you need it in a nutshell:

You must have some increased security on Wordpress; it is very vulnerable to attacks and nasties.

I already gave you advice about selecting usernames and passwords. Add in a nice security plugin, and you've got yourself some decent protection to get you underway.

My tips:

You'll need to navigate to the main plugins area to access the settings for this plugin:

136

Once you click on that **Settings** link, it will open up a long menu on the left-hand side of the page:

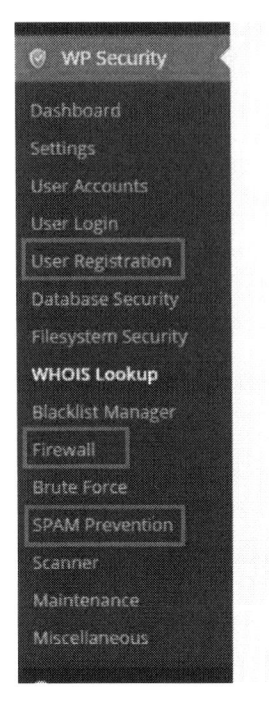

There are many things that we can do to make your Wordpress site more secure using this plugin but, for a beginner's guide, some of them may well confuse you until you've had time to get a little more experience.

So, I've indicated the simplest precautions that you can take for now, without making life difficult for yourself.

In the **User Registration** menu, make sure that these checkboxes are ticked:

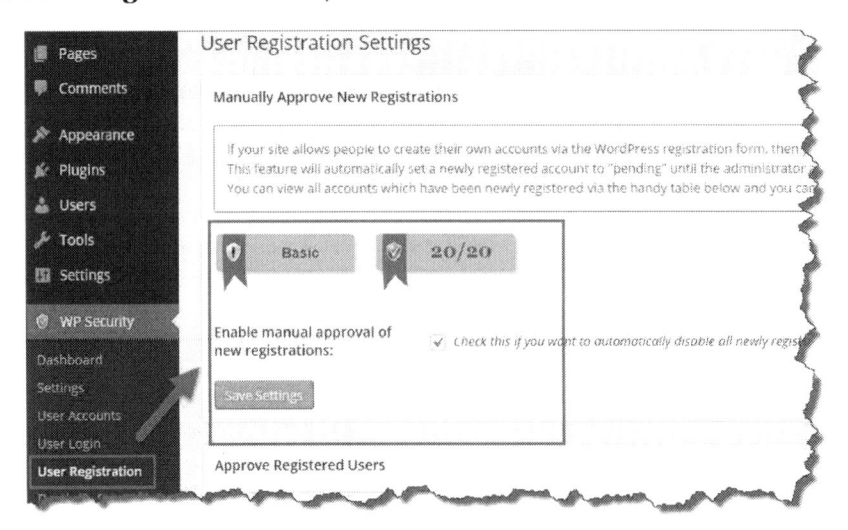

In the **Firewall** menu, make sure that these checkboxes are ticked:

In the **Spam Prevention** menu, make sure that these checkboxes are ticked:

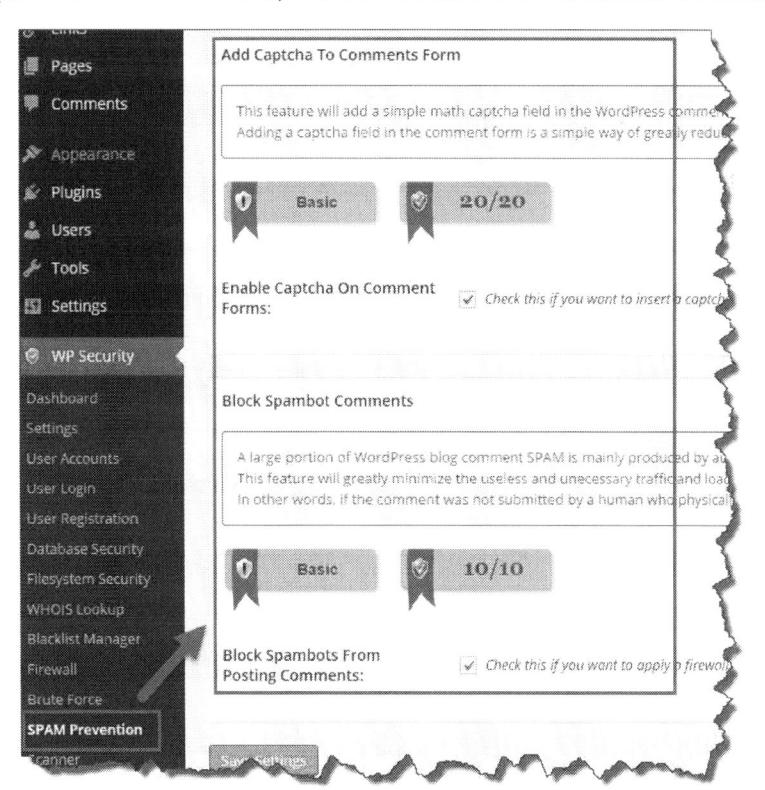

We can *always* improve Wordpress security, but that's a great start, and it won't mess anything up on the site. The security measures will just run quietly in the background.

If do want to dig deeper, head for the main website at https://www.tipsandtricks-hq.com/wordpress-security-and-firewall-plugin.

I actually use Sucuri (at https://sucuri.net/) on my own Wordpress sites because they monitor security on my behalf, and if something goes wrong, they put it right for me.

It's a great service and one that I recommend if your budget stretches to this expense.

Essential Plugin: All in One WP Security & Firewall

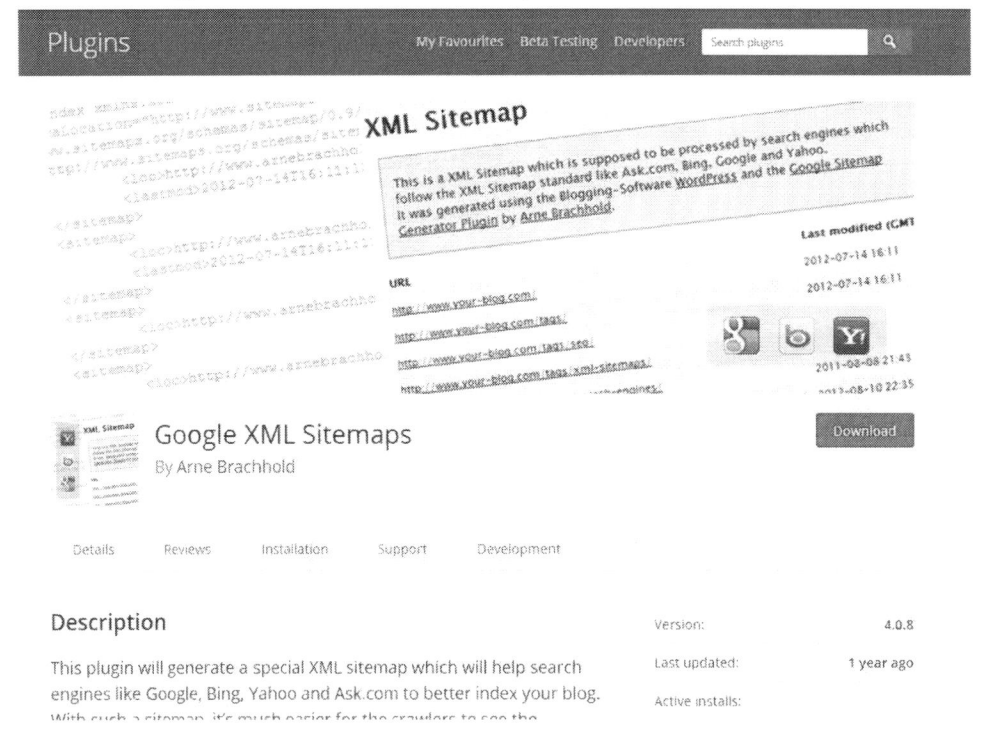

Take a look at https://en-gb.wordpress.org/plugins/google-sitemap-generator/

Full instructions at https://en-gb.wordpress.org/plugins/google-sitemap-generator/#installation

Why you need it in a nutshell:

XML sitemap will help search engines like Google, Bing, Yahoo, and Ask.com to better index your blog.

Additionally, it notifies all major search engines about new content every time you create a post.

In very simple and non-geeky terms, it will make sure that your Wordpress site is found and indexed in the search engines.

Essential Plugins Summary

I don't pretend that this is by any means an exhaustive list of plugins, but it is a great starter pack.

As you learn more about Wordpress, you'll discover new plugins and find ones that you prefer, and hopefully, you'll listen to recommendations from other marketers too.

That's fine, install and remove to suit yourself and *your* blog, keep trying out new plugins and experimenting.

Plugins are easy to install, test and delete and I would always encourage an open mind and a spirit of discovery.

Chapter 11: Wordpress Miscellany

Adding Links to Posts and Pages

We have already touched on Wordpress links, but these have been in relation to our Blogroll

What if you want to add links to a page or post?

It's very easy in Wordpress, all you need to do is to write the text which you wish to link to a post or page:

Next, underline the text that you actually wish to link.

It's usually best for clarity to make it something like Click Here.

Now click the **Insert/Edit Link** icon in the toolbar:

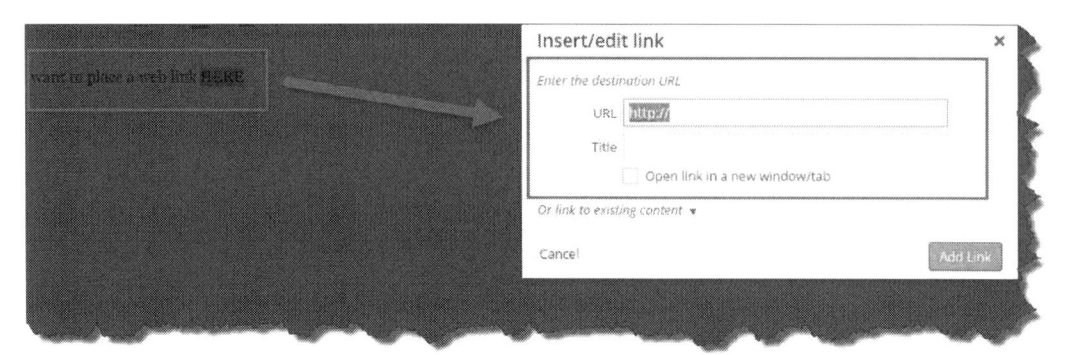

You now need to insert your web link.

Check the box to **Open link in a new window/tab.** This makes for a much better user experience.

Click the **Update** button once you have done that.

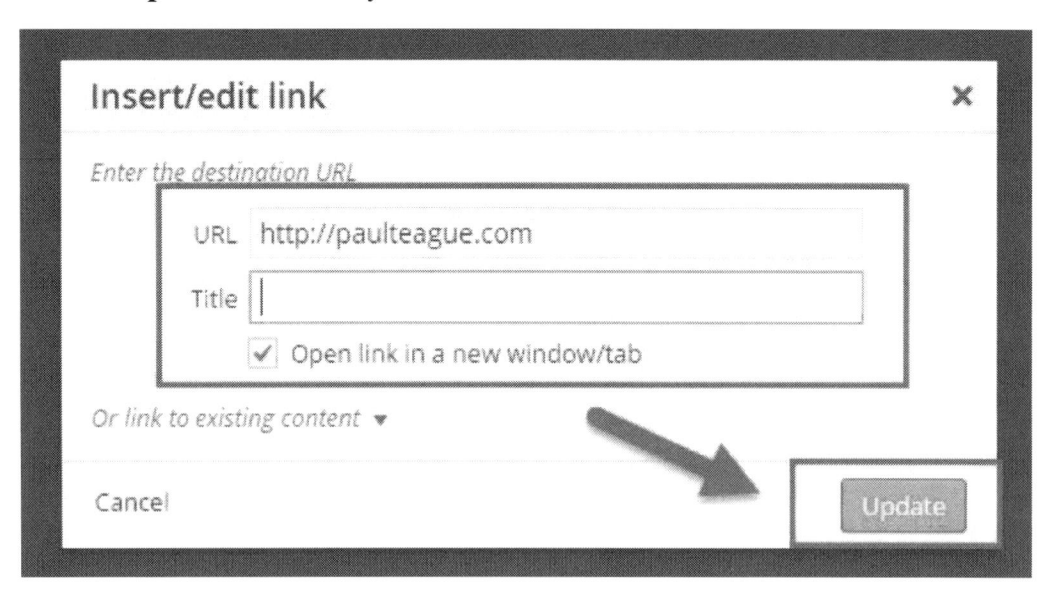

You have now created linked text.

When you publish the post or page and your reader clicks on the underlined/linked word, they will be taken to the URL:

141

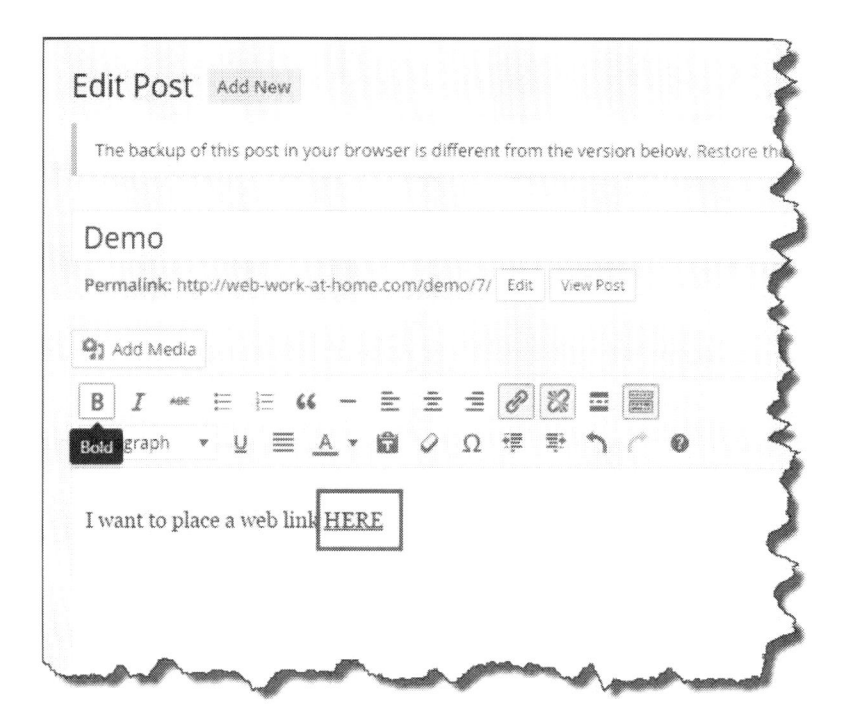

Wordpress Comments

When you create posts, you can choose whether to accept comments or not.

This is generally a good thing, and we have installed Akismet and added Captcha security to the comments form to discourage this from becoming a nuisance.

Wordpress will notify you when you get comments, and you should process them as soon as you can:

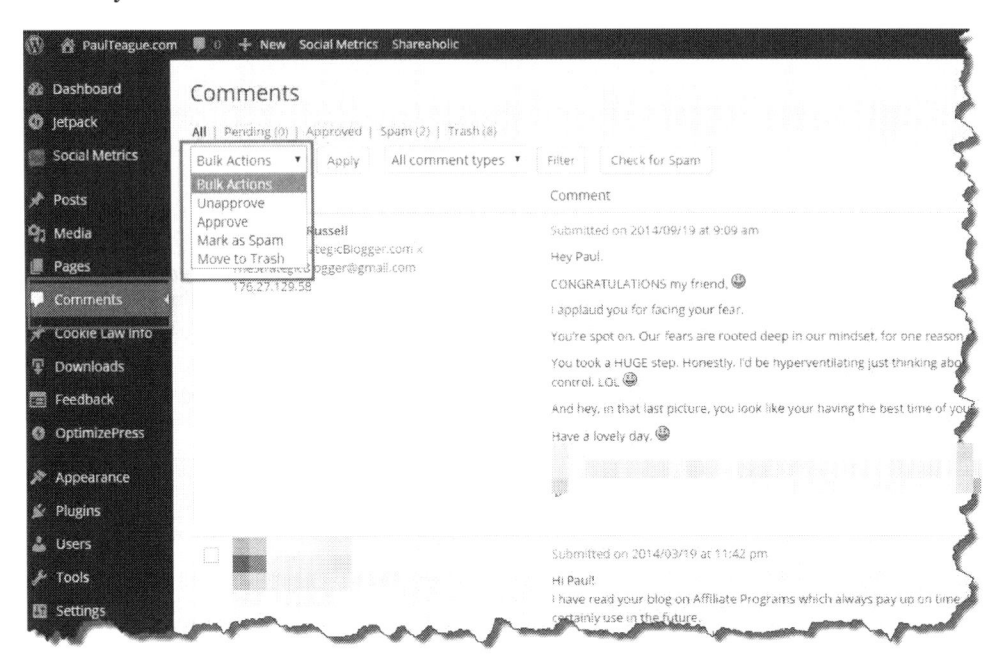

Approve, Mark as Spam, Move to Trash or Unapprove when new comments come in.

You can also **Reply** at the bottom of the comment, and that is a great thing to do because it helps to build a relationship and rapport with your readers.

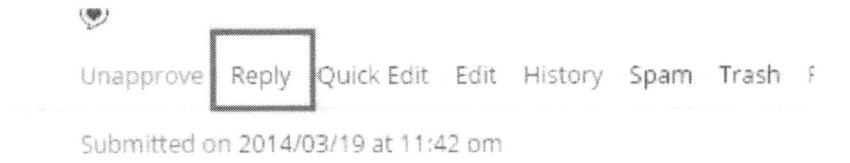

Revisions

Sometimes when working online you can make a right mess of things and you end up wishing that you could go back and start all over again.

The good news is that Wordpress has a solution for that in the form of **Revisions**.

On the right-hand side of any post or page, the **Revisions** option is made available after the second time of saving some content:

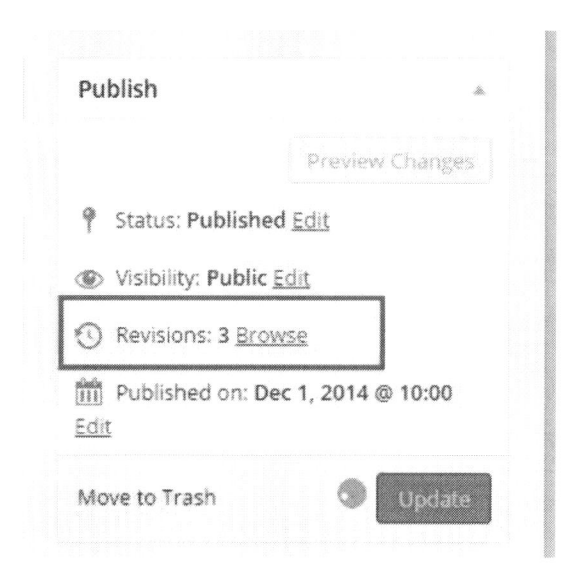

By clicking on the Browse link, you can use the slider in the middle of that page to scroll through previous versions on a post or page.

You can **Compare** any two revisions using the checkbox in the top right-hand corner, and you can click the blue **Restore this revision** button to bring back a previous version:

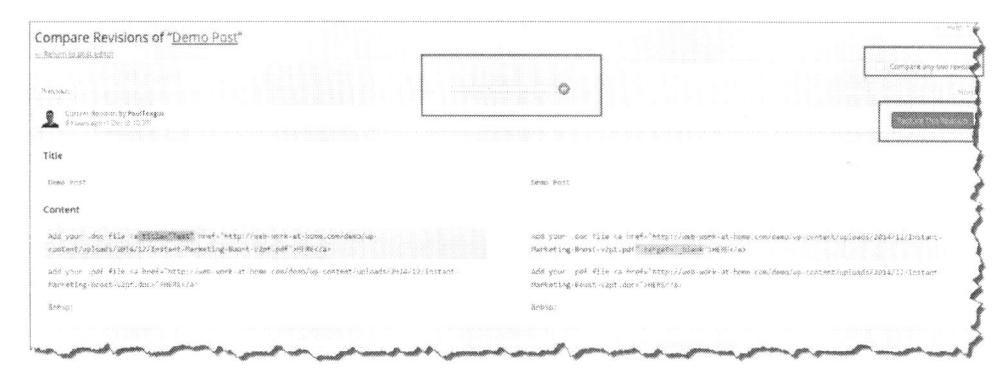

I find this a bit clunky to use, but it has saved my content on quite a few occasions now.

Introduction to Wordpress Widgets

Widgets are very powerful things on a blog, but as a new user to Wordpress, I'm just going to give you the basics here.

Widgets are designated areas on your blog where you can add extra functionality.

On my own blog, the adverts and extras on the right-hand side of my pages are made up of widgets:

144

Those widgets allow me to add social media share code, Amazon books, a search facility and many more great features.

Widget areas depend on the theme that you are using, so the first thing to note is that the widget arrangements in one theme will differ from those in another.

They might be on the left-hand side, the right-hand side, or both.

They might run along the top, the bottom or both.

You access the widgets in two places on the main menu, firstly via the **Appearance** link:

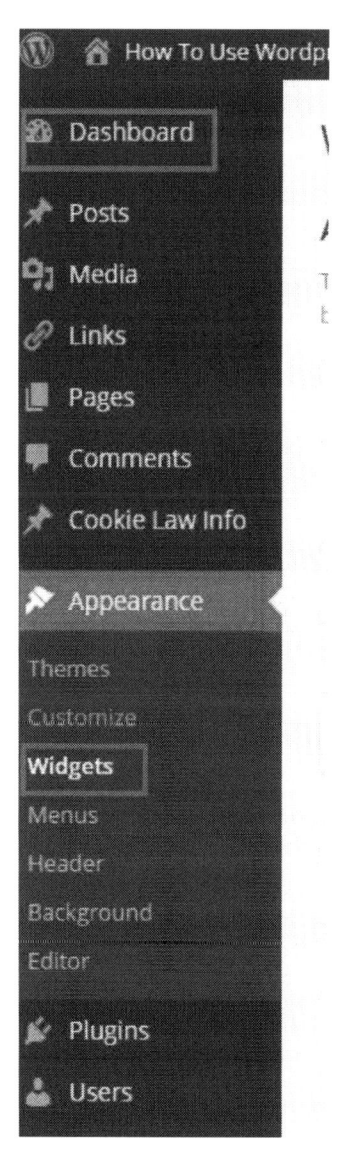

When you click on **Widgets,** you will be able to view and manage the available widgets.

It is also becoming more common to access the widgets via your Wordpress theme, but at the time of writing, it may be one or the other.

For instance, I use the Optimizepress Wordpress theme, and I still access my widgets via the menu shown above. They are not available to me using the second method.

The second method of accessing widgets is via the main menu, but using the Themes customization area:

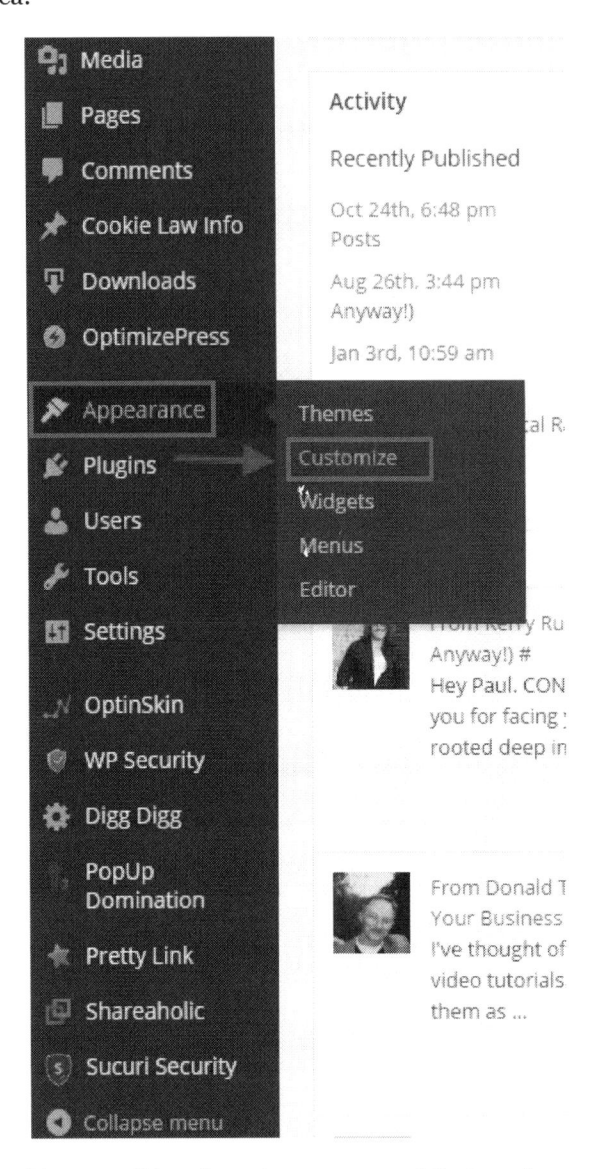

Unfortunately, at this stage, I just have to recommend that you're aware of both techniques because the one you use will depend very much on the theme that you have installed.

So, for now, just be aware that either – or even both – methods may actually work for you.

The important thing is that you know where to find everything.

I'm hoping that Wordpress will add some uniformity to widgets in a future upgrade.

Once you click on Appearance/Customize as in the image on the previous page, the widgets will look a little different using this method:

The principles are exactly the same.

However, only your widget areas appear on the left-hand side (1). You can search for the widget that you want to use (2), and your installed widgets are all lined up on the right-hand side (3):

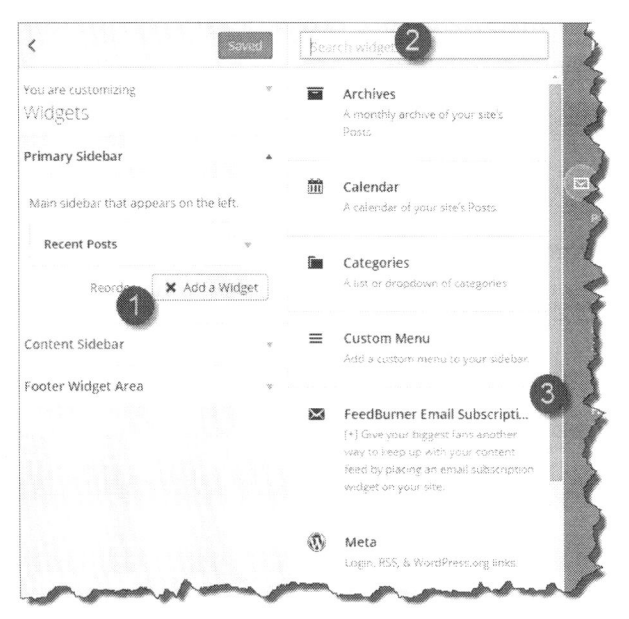

I have indicated the best widgets to use as a new user:

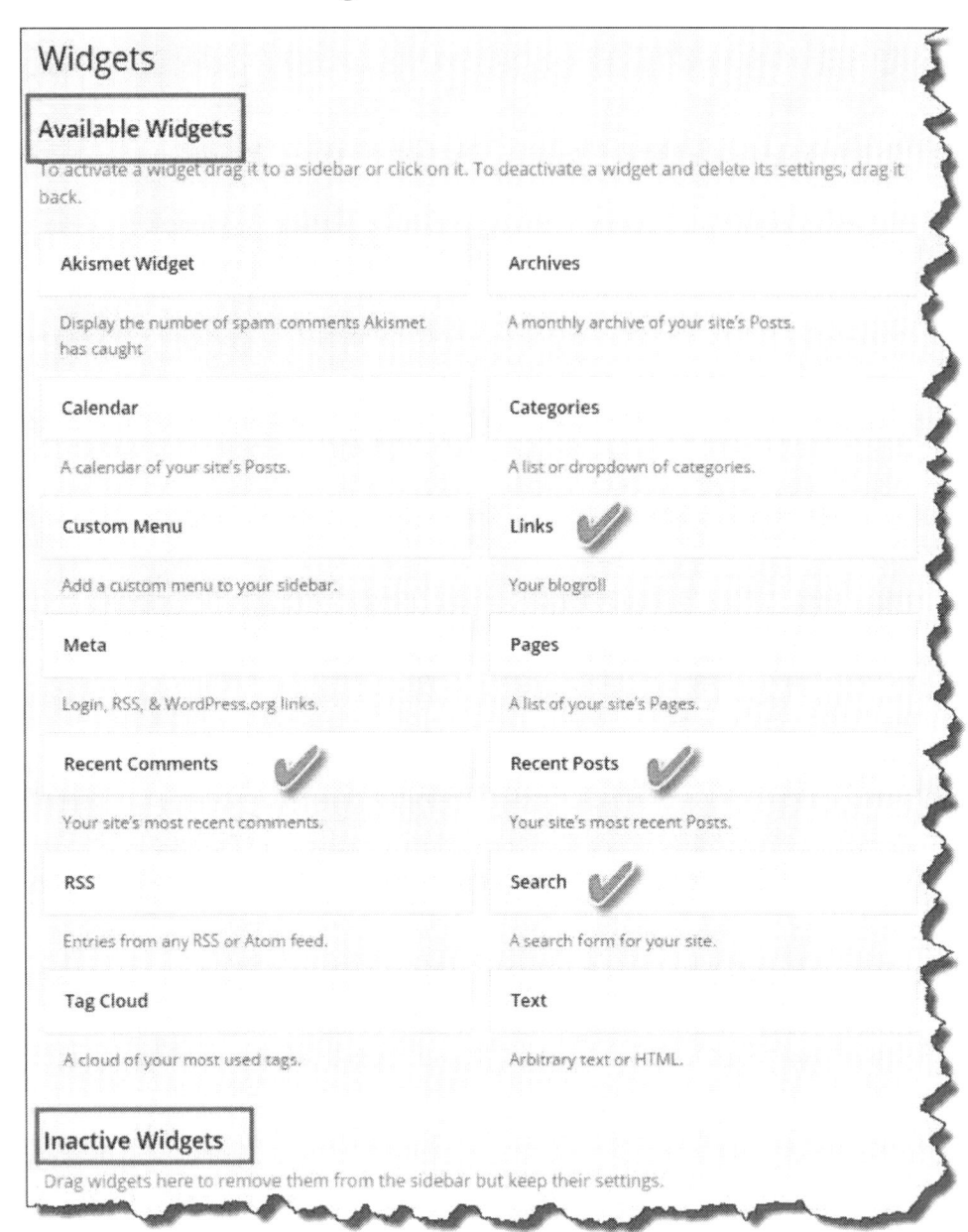

Widgets

Available Widgets

To activate a widget drag it to a sidebar or click on it. To deactivate a widget and delete its settings, drag it back.

Akismet Widget	**Archives**
Display the number of spam comments Akismet has caught	A monthly archive of your site's Posts.
Calendar	**Categories**
A calendar of your site's Posts.	A list or dropdown of categories.
Custom Menu	**Links** ✓
Add a custom menu to your sidebar.	Your blogroll
Meta	**Pages**
Login, RSS, & WordPress.org links.	A list of your site's Pages.
Recent Comments ✓	**Recent Posts** ✓
Your site's most recent comments.	Your site's most recent Posts.
RSS	**Search** ✓
Entries from any RSS or Atom feed.	A search form for your site.
Tag Cloud	**Text**
A cloud of your most used tags.	Arbitrary text or HTML.

Inactive Widgets

Drag widgets here to remove them from the sidebar but keep their settings.

On the right-hand side of the widgets page, you will see how your widgets are allocated in your theme.

You can move the widgets up and down, drag them to the **Inactive Widgets** area and drag and drop new widgets from the **Available Widgets** area:

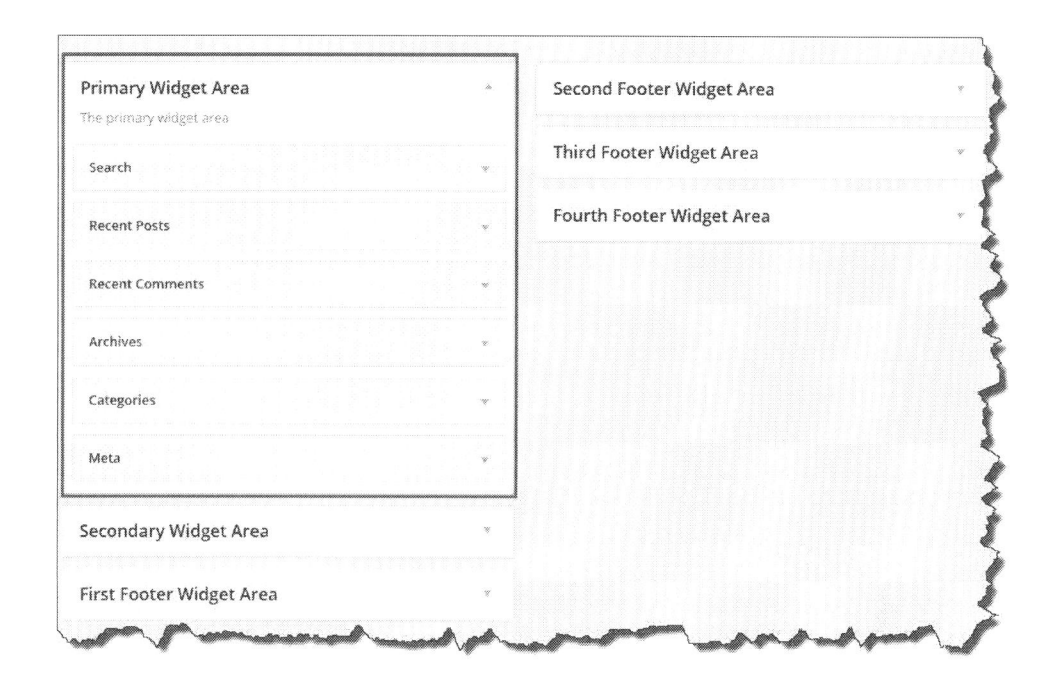

If you wish to delete any particular widget, click the little arrows on the right-hand side (see below) and click on the **Delete** link:

That's very much the basics of widgets. They can be very useful and powerful tools, but that's all best saved for now for a more advanced look at Wordpress.

Introduction to Wordpress Menus

The final skill that you need to master as a Wordpress beginner is **Menus**.

These are found via Dashboard – Appearance – Menus in the main navigation:

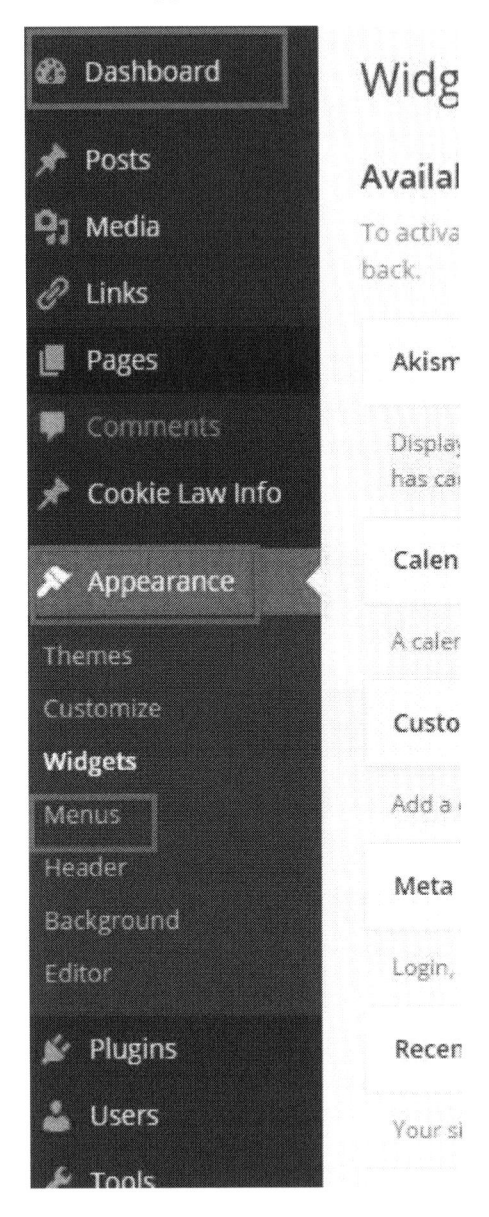

As with widgets, we can get very adventurous with menus, but in this book I'm just going to give you the survival basics.

You will have been given a ready-made menu already, and it probably has something fairly basic on it to start with:

Mainly you will add Pages and Links to the menu.

To add pages (see 1 in the image below) check the box next to the page that you want to add to the menu, then click the grey **Add to Menu** button.

You can drag and drop items in the **Menu Structure** up and down.

To add links to a menu - maybe you have a Helpdesk link as I do - click on the little downwards arrow to the right of **Links** (as shown in 2 in the above image).

Enter your URL, complete the Link Text box and click the grey **Add To Menu** button.

You must click the **Save Menu** button once you have completed your menu changes. Otherwise, it will not be saved:

You can get quite ambitious with menus and run multiple menus across your blog, but that is really all you need to know about menus to get started.

Depending on your theme, you may also have to designate a menu location - usually something like 'Top of page,' 'Bottom of page', or similar.

Chapter 12: Other Useful Things To Do In Siteground

When you set up your blog, there are a couple of extra things that you might as well do.

They're simple enough, and you've paid for them as part of the service – so why not?

Set Up Your Personalised Email Address

First of all, it's great for branding to have an email address which corresponds to your domain name.

So, if your domain name is fabthings.com, you might want to set up email addresses like fred@fabthings.com or info@fabthings.com

This is easy to do and free within your Siteground cPanel (this is your Control Panel, remember)

To get started, you will need to login to Siteground:

Once you are logged on, click on **My Accounts**:

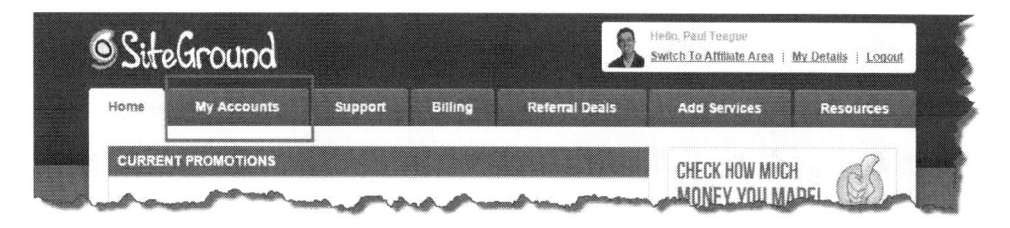

Next, click on the **Manage Account** button.

Remember, your account will look different from mine as I host two accounts on Siteground:

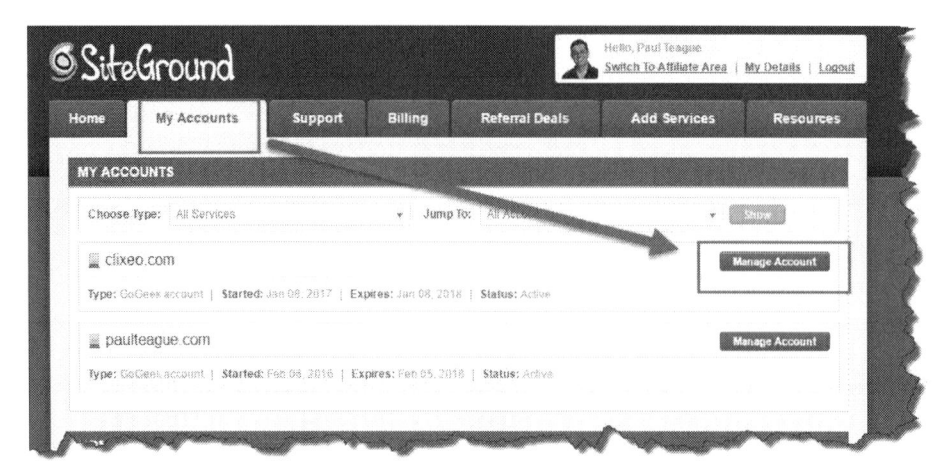

Finally, click on the orange cPanel button to take you to the main admin area for your account:

Navigate towards the lower part of the cPanel area until you find the section which contains **MAIL**:

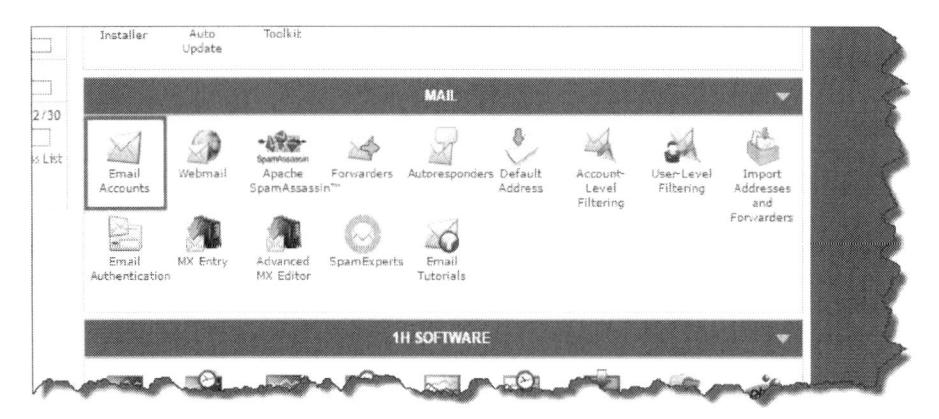

Click on the **Email Accounts** icon, as shown in the image on the previous page.

In the area shown below, you can now create as many personalised emails as you wish.

However, just because you can doesn't mean that you should!

A couple of bespoke email addresses will be fine – don't get carried away.

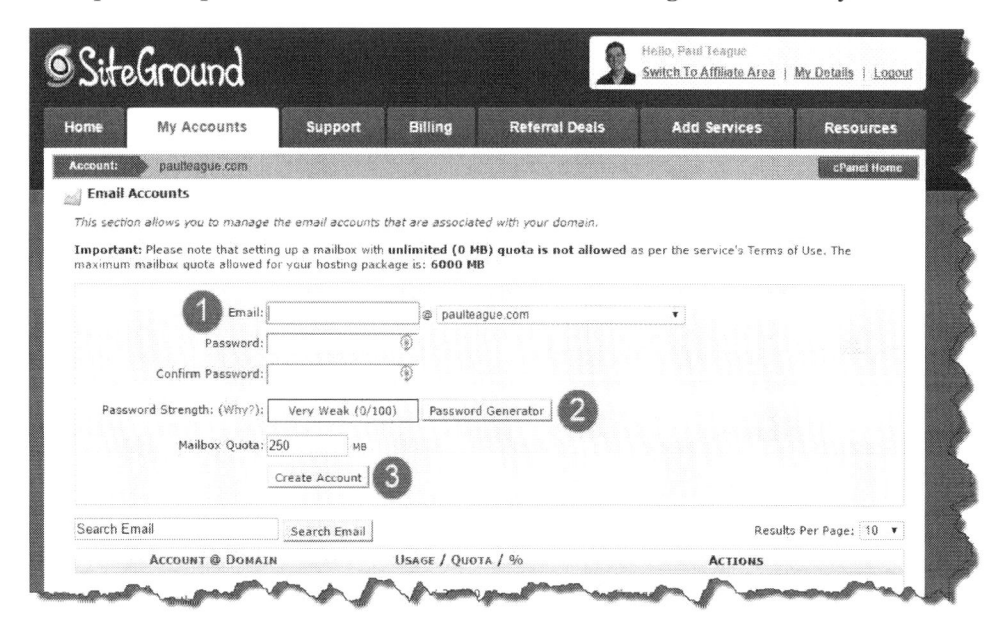

In the image above:

1 – Enter whatever you want your email address to be.

In this example, it's going to be in the format XYZ@paulteague.com

I'd recommend that you go for your first name.

2 – Once you've done that, click the **Password Generator** button.

I'm going to show you how to set up these emails simply, so we won't actually use the password in this scenario.

Just generate the password - you don't need to write it down - and move on.

3 – To create your new email account, just click on that **Create Account** button.

Although your new email address is now created, it doesn't actually go anywhere yet.

You can use a system which requires things like POP3 and SMTP settings.

This is the next level of geekiness, so I'm going to avoid it in this book.

For now, just create whichever email addresses you want to use in your business:

Account @ Domain	Usage / Quota / %	Actions			
admin@thesecretbunker.net	2 / 250.00 MB	Change Password	Change Quota	Delete	More
admin@self-publishing-journeys.com	0 / 250.00 MB	Change Password	Change Quota	Delete	More
admin@paulteague.com	0 / 250.00 MB	Change Password	Change Quota	Delete	More
affiliate@paulteague.com	0 / 250.00 MB	Change Password	Change Quota	Delete	More
author@paulteague.com	0 / 250.00 MB	Change Password	Change Quota	Delete	More
...ook@paulteague.com	0 / 250.00 MB	Change	Change	Delete	More

To avoid getting involved with POP3 and SMTP settings, we're just going to forward all these emails to your regular account at Gmail, Outlook.com or whatever service you use.

To set this up, head back to that **MAIL** area in cPanel.

Click on the icon marked **Forwarders**.

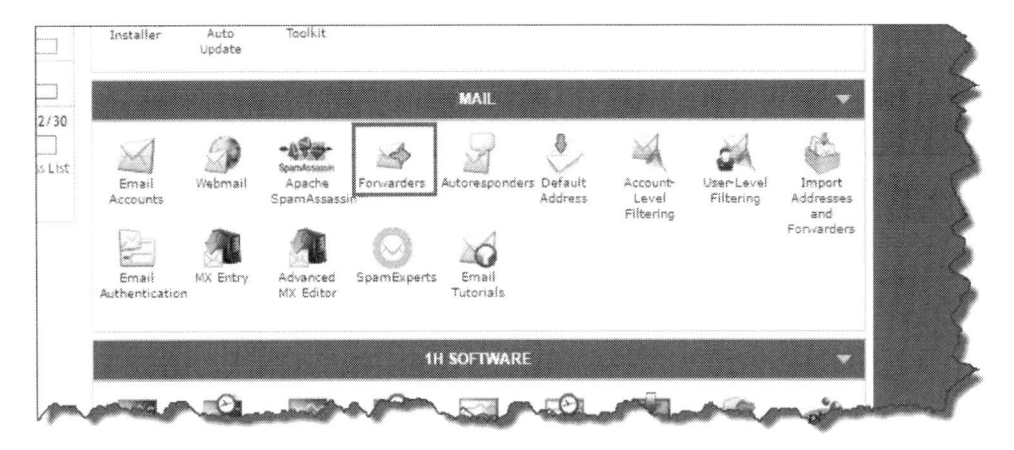

In this area, you can set every one of your new email addresses to automatically forward to the email address that you use every day.

Although I know how to set up POP3 and SMTP settings, I still use this forwarding system for convenience on addresses that I don't use so often.

There's no technical hassle involved, which is why I'm recommending it to you.

In the image on the next page, you can see how I have set up all of my bespoke email addresses to forward to my Gmail address:

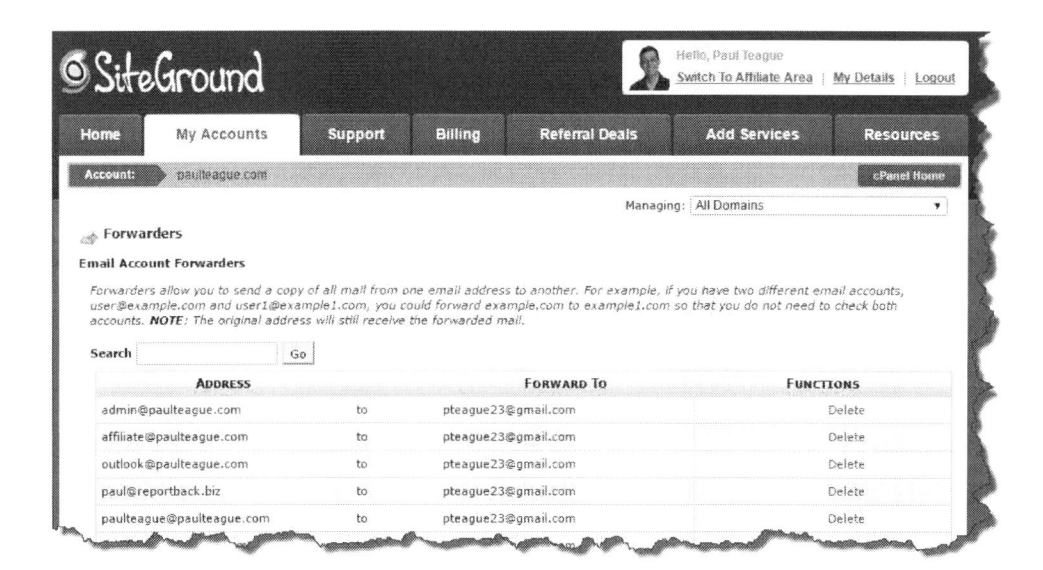

To set this up for each of the email addresses that you created, follow the steps shown in the image below:

1 – Enter the email identifier, i.e., fred, admin, info, etc.

2 – Enter the email address that you want to forward your emails to.

3 – Click on the **Add Forwarder** button.

That's it; you can now use those new, bespoke email addresses wherever you want to and, when somebody sends an email to one of them, it will automatically forward to the email address that you use every day.

It's not perfect, but it is simple and does, at least, allow you to use branded emails.

SSL To Make Google Happy

Without wanting to 'over-geek' you, Google is now showing a preference to websites which use https rather than http.

There is a full article explaining this move at https://webmasters.googleblog.com/2014/08/https-as-ranking-signal.html.

You'll already be familiar with banks and payment checkouts having https and a green padlock displayed in your browser when you use them.

Well, this is the same - at a lesser level of encryption, but much more secure for users.

In simple terms, like a blog or website host, you need to make the switch.

Google has clearly signalled the standard that it expects of website owners and you can ignore it at your peril or just get on with the job.

The good news for you, as a Siteground user, is that this is free for you and only takes a couple of minutes.

It's built into their basic hosting service, and I highly recommend that you activate it as soon as you start work on your Wordpress site.

We're going to repeat the process that we just used to set-up emails in cPanel.

To get started, you will need to login to Siteground:

Once you are logged on, click on **My Accounts**:

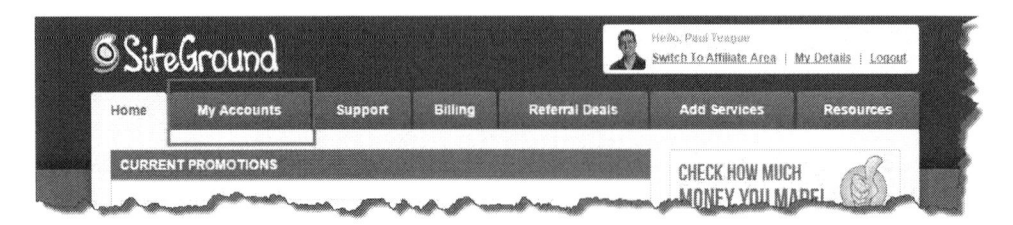

Next, click on the **Manage Account** button.

Remember, your account will look different from mine as I host two accounts on Siteground:

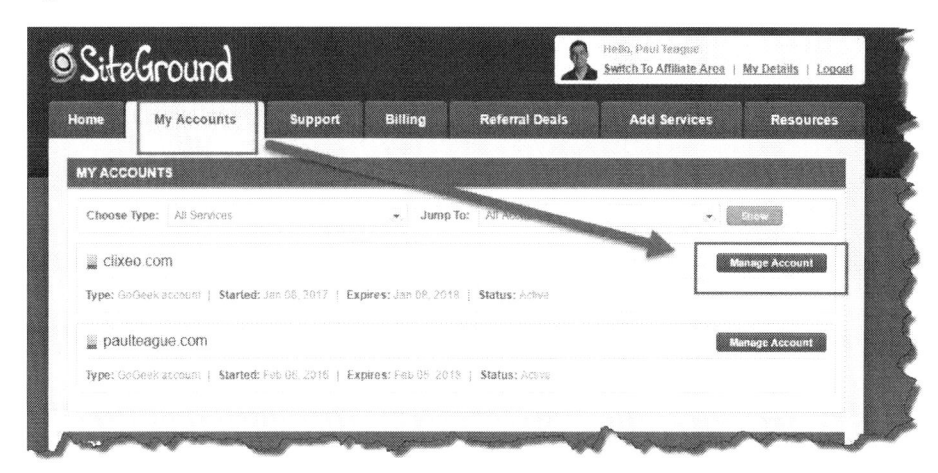

You now need to click on the **Extra Services** tab, as shown below:

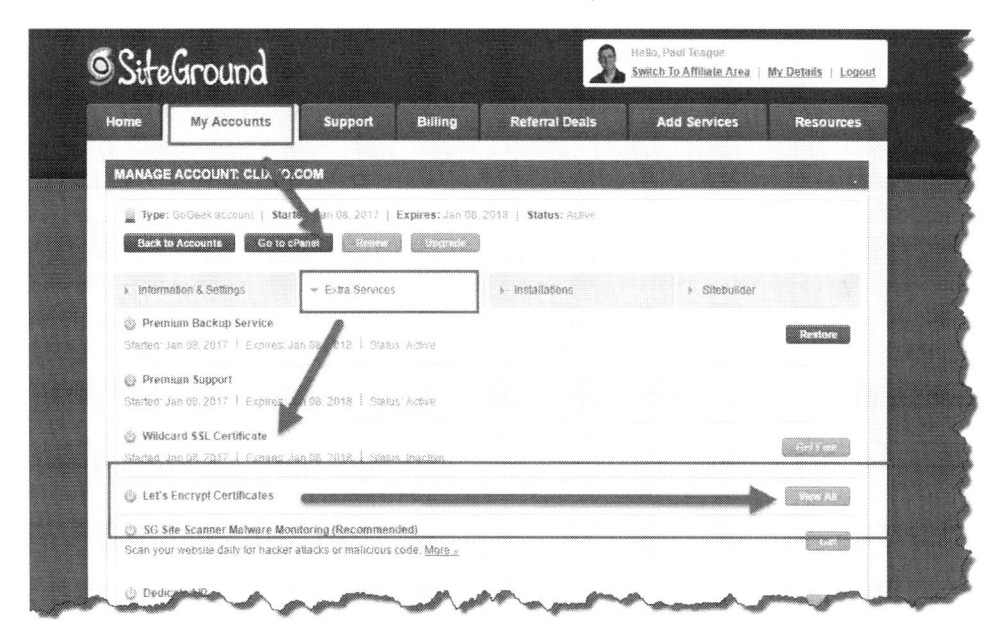

This is a little different now from setting up emails because we're not working in the cPanel area this time around.

You need to navigate to **Let's Encrypt Certificates**, as shown above.

Click on the green **View All** button.

Siteground allows you to install free SSL certificates which will change your website URL from http:// to https://

Normally this is pretty complicated, but Siteground makes life really easy for us.

At the bottom of this area, you will see that you can **Install new Let's Encrypt Certificate** via the simple interface:

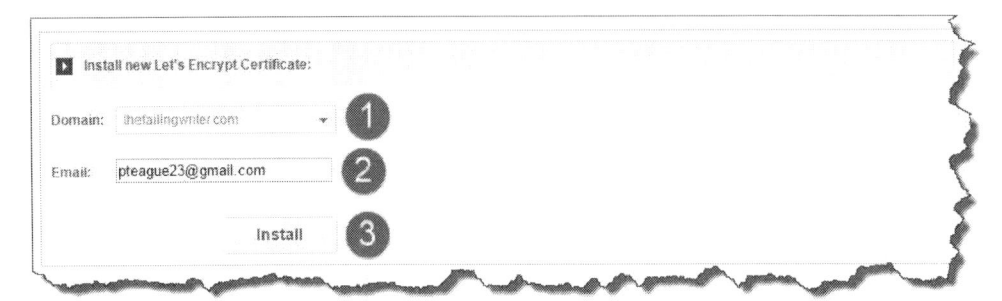

1 – Select your domain name.

If you only have one, this is straightforward. If you have more than one, select them one at a time via the drop-down menu.

2 – Select an email address for your confirmation.

3 – Click the **Install** button.

You're done!

Your new Wordpress site is now fully compliant with Google's requirements at the time of writing.

This puts you way ahead of your competitors, most of whom haven't a clue that this is even a requirement!

What Next with Wordpress?

Congratulations!

You now understand all the basics of Wordpress.

In fact, you're way ahead of most beginners.

You've actually done some very advanced stuff in this book though hopefully, you weren't really aware of it at the time.

We've set up a great starter blog, and we've done it in a way that you can grow, develop and build without having to throw out anything that you have created at a later stage.

We've paid attention to security, Search Engine Optimization and all of the core features of Wordpress.

All you have to do now is to get writing.

Create your About Me, Contact Me, Terms and Conditions and Privacy Policy pages and add them to your menu.

You might even wish to grab a free Helpdesk with Freshdesk at https://freshdesk.com/helpdesk-system and add a link to it via your Menu.

I would now encourage you to get writing and start experimenting with Wordpress.

Take it out for a spin.

As you've seen, it's very difficult to actually break it.

I have used Wordpress for many years now, and I hope this guide will empower you to do exactly the same thing in your business for years to come.

Paul Teage

Great Wordpress Resources

Here are some recommended resources to support your learning of Wordpress and also to encourage you to take your learning to the next stage:

WordPress.com at https://wordpress.com/

WordPress.org at https://wordpress.org/

The difference between a blog and a website at https://www.shoutmeloud.com/difference-between-blog-vs-website.html

WordPress support at https://wordpress.org/support/

WordPress forums at http://en.forums.wordpress.com/forum/support

Learn WordPress at https://learn.wordpress.com/

Free WordPress hosting at 000webhost at https://www.000webhost.com

SiteGround dedicated Wordpress hosting at https://www.siteground.com/wordpress-hosting.htm

Sucuri WordPress site monitoring at https://sucuri.net/

ManageWP for multiple WordPress sites at https://managewp.com/

About The Author

Hi, I'm **Paul Teague,** and I've been making websites since 2001.

In my professional life, my team and I won an international Webby Award in the 'Communities section' during 2006; an award won by Flickr the year after.

In 2009, we followed that up with Silver in the W³ Awards.

I run numerous websites, but you should check out my blog at PaulTeague.com first of all as that's where I place all my free information, tips and content about working online.

You can also connect with me easily via social media on that site.

Although I write mainly fiction books, I also some non-fiction titles listed as P Teague.

I teach social and digital marketing topics to corporate clients through my local Chamber of Commerce and speak on web marketing topics to organisations such as The Society of Authors, The Alliance of Independent Authors and Amazon Academy.

I have written two sci-fi/dystopian trilogies - The Secret Bunker Trilogy and The Grid Trilogy - and you can find out more about them at my author website: https://paulteague.net/

I also write psychological thrillers as Paul J. Teague, and you can find out more about them at https://paulteague.co.uk/

Other Resources from Paul Teague

Check out my most recommended web tools at https://wp-unboxed.com/Recommended.

I use – or have used - all of these resources in my business, many of them every day.

I hope that they are useful to you.

As a thank you for buying 'Wordpress Unboxed, I'd like to give you a complimentary copy of the book to download in .pdf format so that you may refer to it when setting up your own Wordpress blog.

It will be easier to access the web links in the .pdf version, and you may also wish to download it to your PC or laptop.

To access the .pdf version, please go to:

https://wp-unboxed.com/unboxed

Enjoy!

Paul Teague

WORDPRESS UNBOXED VIDEO

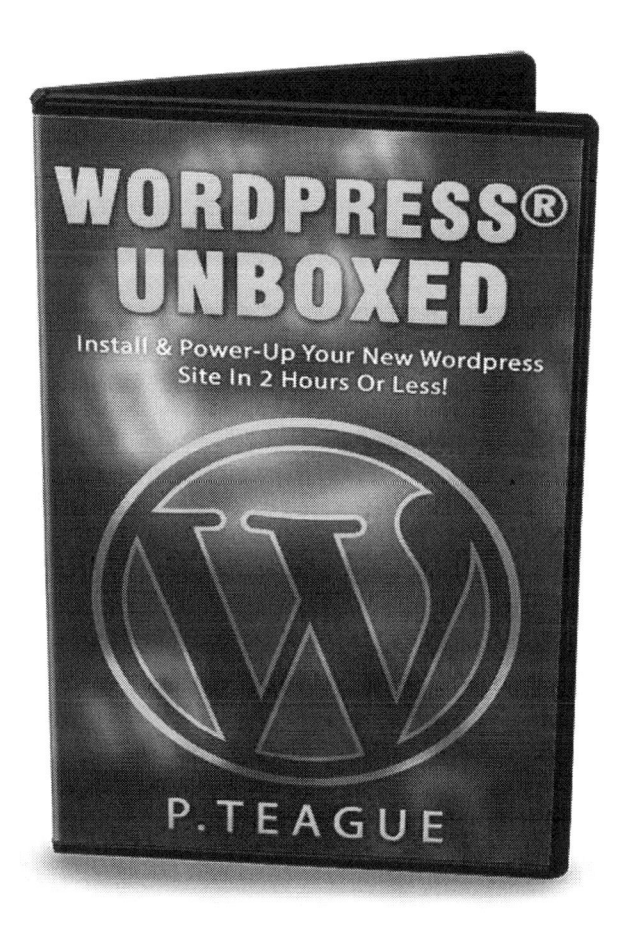

Grab your free 1-hour Wordpress video walk-through at

https://wp-unboxed.com/FREE

Paul Teague's Blog

Check it out at:

https://paulteague.com/

Brought to you by

WORDPRESS UNBOXED

THE SIMPLE, JARGON-FREE GUIDE TO SETTING UP YOUR FIRST WORDPRESS WEBSITE

P. Teague

Copyright © 2017 by Paul Teague (writing as P.Teague) & Clixeo Publishing

No part of this book may be reproduced, stored in retrieval systems, or transmitted by any means, electronic, mechanical, photocopying, recorded or otherwise without written permission from the author.

Disclaimer

Some of the services recommended in this book will earn me a small affiliate income if you click on certain links and go on to purchase. I only recommend products and services which I personally use. Please read my disclosure notice at http://www.clixeo.com/disclosure/ for full information.

All of the information in this book was up to date at the time of publication. Due to the ever-changing nature of the web, some of the screen shots may differ slightly from what you see in your own account. ***Please note that this book is sold as-is, without the provision or expectation of support or technical assistance.***

Wordpress is a registered Trademark of The Wordpress Foundation, which does not endorse, support or sponsor the content of this book in any way. All opinions expressed are those of the author.

Printed in Great Britain
by Amazon